Developing Num...

SOLVING PROBLEMS

ACTIVITIES FOR THE DAILY MATHS LESSON

year 2

Hilary Koll and Steve Mills

A & C BLACK

Contents

Reprinted 2001, 2002 (twice), 2003, 2004, 2005, 2006, 2007, 2008, 2009, 2011
Published 2000 by A & C Black Publishers Limited
36 Soho Square, London W1D 3QY
www.acblack.com

ISBN 978-0-7136-5445-5
Copyright text © Hilary Koll and Steve Mills, 2000
Copyright illustrations © Kirsty Wilson, 2000
Copyright cover illustration © Charlotte Hard, 2000
Editors: Lynne Williamson and Marie Lister

The authors and publishers would like to thank the following teachers for their advice in producing this series of books:
Stuart Anslow; Jane Beynon; Cathy Davey; Ann Flint; Shirley Gooch; Barbara Locke; Madeleine Madden; Helen Mason;
Fern Oliver; Jo Turpin.
A CIP catalogue record for this book is available from the British Library.

A & C Black uses paper produced with elemental chlorine-free pulp, harvested from managed sustainable forests.

Printed and bound in Great Britain

Introduction

Developing Numeracy: Solving Problems is a series of seven photocopiable activity books designed to be used during the daily maths lesson. They focus on the third strand of the National Numeracy Strategy *Framework for teaching mathematics*. The activities are intended to be used in the time allocated to pupil activities; they aim to reinforce the knowledge, understanding and skills taught during the main part of the lesson and to provide practice and consolidation of the objectives contained in the framework document.

Year 2 supports the teaching of mathematics by providing a series of activities which develop essential skills in solving mathematical problems. On the whole the activities are designed for children to work on independently, although this is not always possible and occasionally some children may need support.

Year 2 encourages children to

- choose and use appropriate operations and efficient calculation strategies to solve problems;
- solve mathematical problems and puzzles and to explore relationships and patterns;
- investigate a general statement about familiar numbers or shapes;
- explain how a problem was solved;
- solve one-step and two-step worded problems in areas of 'real life', money and measures;
- recognise all coins and begin to use £.p notation;
- solve problems by organising and using data.

Extension

Many of the activity sheets end with a challenge (**Now try this!**) which reinforces and extends the children's learning, and provides the teacher with the opportunity for assessment. On occasion you may wish to read out the instructions and explain the activity before the children begin working on it. The children may need to record their answers on a separate piece of paper.

Differentiated activities

For some activities, two differentiated versions are provided which have the same title and are presented on facing pages in the book. On the left is the less challenging activity, indicated by a rocket icon: . The more challenging version is found on the right, indicated by a shooting star: . These activity sheets could be given to different groups within the class, or all the children could complete the first sheet and children requiring further extension could then be given the second sheet.

Organisation

Very little equipment is needed, but it will be useful to have available: coloured pencils, interlocking cubes, counters, scissors, number lines, digit cards, real or plastic coins. You will need to provide dice for page 21, and small clocks for pages 52–53 if desired.

To help teachers to select appropriate learning experiences for the children, the activities are grouped into sections within each book. However, the activities are not expected to be used in that order unless otherwise stated. The sheets are intended to support, rather than direct, the teacher's planning.

Some activities can be made easier or more challenging by masking and substituting some of the numbers. You may wish to re-use some pages by copying them onto card and laminating them, or by enlarging them onto A3 paper.

Teachers' notes

Very brief notes are provided at the foot of each page giving ideas and suggestions for maximising the effectiveness of the activity sheets. These can be masked before copying.

Structure of the daily maths lesson

The recommended structure of the daily maths lesson for Key Stage 1 is as follows:

Start to lesson, oral work, mental calculation	5–10 minutes
Main teaching and pupil activities *(the activities in the **Developing Numeracy** books are designed to be carried out in the time allocated to pupil activities)*	about 30 minutes
Plenary *(whole-class review and consolidation)*	about 10 minutes

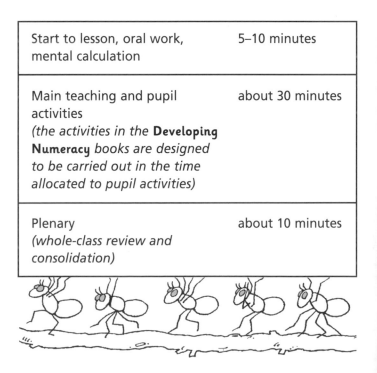

Whole-class activities

The following activities provide some practical ideas which can be used to introduce or reinforce the main teaching part of the lesson.

Making decisions

Number question strip

On a strip of card or thick paper write a number fact, for example *10 + 5 = 15*. Wrap a narrow piece of paper around the strip of card so that it can slide sideways to mask one of the numbers or operator signs. Hold up the strip and ask the children to find the hidden number or sign. This can then be revealed to check that it is correct. You could build up a collection of number strips to use throughout the year.

Classroom sorting

Count the number of children in the class. Select individuals to sort the children in the class into sets, for example, brown eyes/blue eyes, trousers/skirts. Ask questions about each set, such as: *How many children have blue eyes? How many more/fewer children have brown eyes than blue eyes? How would you work out the answer to this question? Can you write it as a number statement, using figures?*

Reasoning about numbers

Counting stick

You will need a stick which is divided into ten equal coloured sections (such as a metre stick with each 10 cm coloured). Hold the stick so that all the children can see it and point to each section along it in turn. Decide on a number (for example, two) and ask the children to counts in twos as you point to each section. This provides practice in counting forwards and backwards and helps the children to remember the multiples of the given number. Odd and even numbers can be explored in this way, beginning with any odd or even number.

Double, double trouble

Choose a start number and then call out doubling and halving instructions, for example: *Begin with two. Double it, double it, halve it, double it. Which number are you on now?*

As a variation, you could give a range of addition, subtraction, multiplication or division instructions, for example: *Add three, multiply by two.*

Reasoning about shapes

I spy

Find shapes in and around the classroom, or shapes which can be seen from the classroom window. Begin by saying: *I spy a shape on the wall with three pointed corners. What shape is it? I spy a cuboid in our classroom. What am I looking at? I spy the clock on the wall. What shape is it?* etc.

Problems involving 'real life'

Moving around the classroom

Ask the children to estimate the number of paces that a child should move from a marked spot (for example, the waste bin) to different objects in the classroom (such as the door). Choose a child to test the estimates, and ask questions such as: *Is that far enough/too far? How many more steps are needed? Whose guess was the nearest?* Extend this idea to longer distances, for example: *How many paces do you think it will take you to walk from here to the climbing frame?* As an extension, 'pigeon steps' can be used instead of paces.

Problems involving money

I started with...

Begin by saying: *I started with 20p and bought something for 2p. Then I had 18p left.* Point to another child to continue: *I started with 18p and bought something for 1p. Then I had 17p left.* If correct, that child chooses another child to continue. Tell the children that they may not spend more than 4p at a time. When no money is left, start again at 20p.

Problems involving measures

Mass guess

Show the children two boxes of a similar size. One box should contain something heavy, for example, a kilogram weight, and the other something lighter. Ask the children: *Do you think these boxes weigh the same? Can you tell, just by looking, which box is heavier?*

Show a third box, larger and lighter than the other two, for example, an empty cereal packet.
Ask the children: *Which do you think is heaviest? Are big things always heavier than smaller things?*

Invite several children to feel the boxes and continue: *Can anyone think of something that is very large but very light? Or something that is small but very heavy?* Discuss the children's suggestions.

Make it up

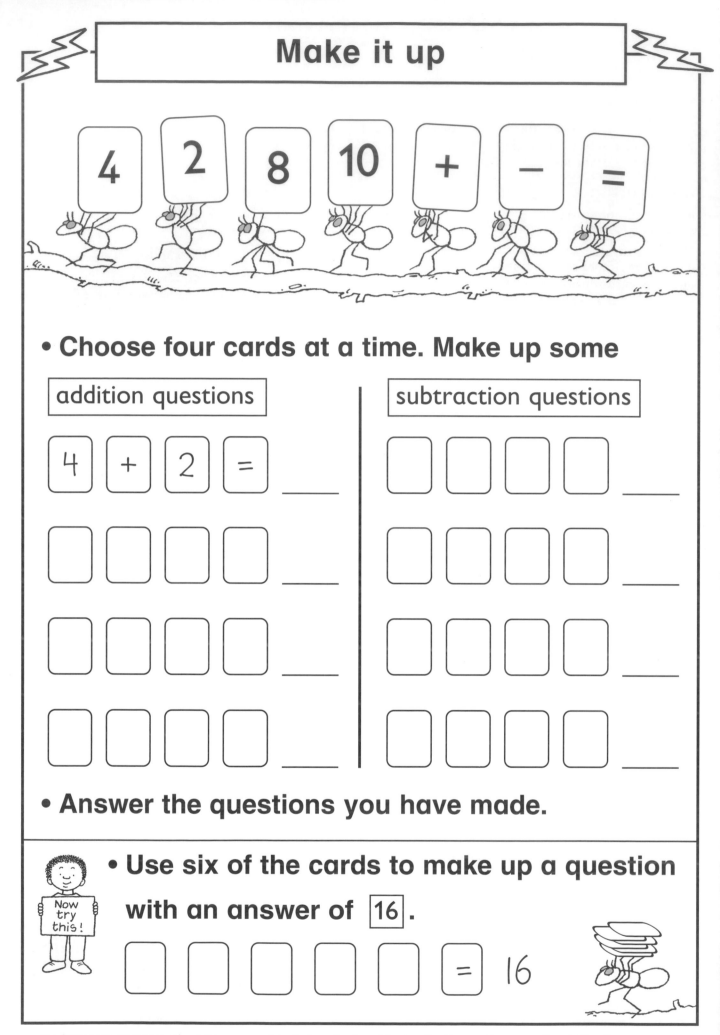

| 4 | 2 | 8 | 10 | + | − | = |

- **Choose four cards at a time. Make up some**

addition questions	subtraction questions

4 + 2 = __

☐ ☐ ☐ ☐ __

☐ ☐ ☐ ☐ __

☐ ☐ ☐ ☐ __

☐ ☐ ☐ ☐ __

☐ ☐ ☐ ☐ __

☐ ☐ ☐ ☐ __

☐ ☐ ☐ ☐ __

- **Answer the questions you have made.**

Now try this!

- **Use six of the cards to make up a question with an answer of 16 .**

☐ ☐ ☐ ☐ ☐ = 16

Teachers' note Encourage the children to explain their methods and to describe the questions using a range of vocabulary, for example: plus, add, altogether, minus, take away, subtract. Some children may find digit cards useful for this activity.

**Developing Numeracy
Solving Problems Year 2
© A & C Black**

Warm up and work out!

- **Work out the answers.**
- **Show your workings on the mats.**

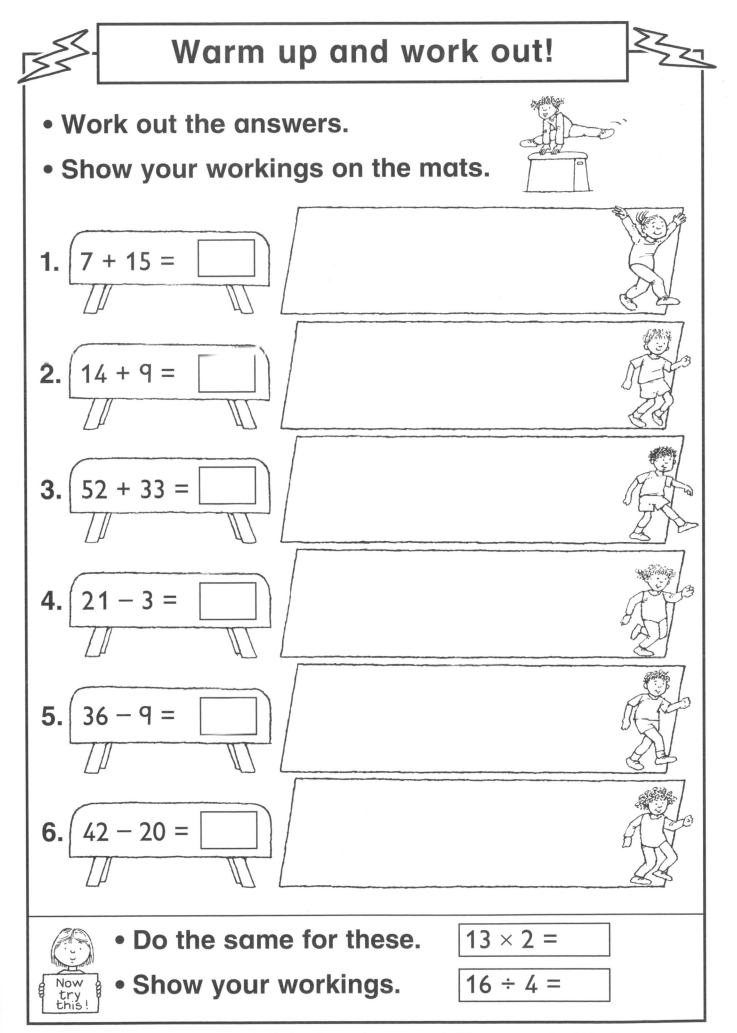

1. 7 + 15 =

2. 14 + 9 =

3. 52 + 33 =

4. 21 − 3 =

5. 36 − 9 =

6. 42 − 20 =

- **Do the same for these.**   13 × 2 =
- **Show your workings.**   16 ÷ 4 =

Now try this!

Teachers' note The questions can be masked before photocopying to create a flexible resource. To make the activity simpler, write only addition questions, or a mixture of easier addition and subtraction questions, on the sheet.

Developing Numeracy
Solving Problems Year 2
© A & C Black

Farmyard fun

- **Write a number statement for each number story.**

Example: I have 12p. I spend 7p.
I have 5p left.

$12 - 7 = 5$

Sheep have 4 legs.
3 sheep have 12 legs
altogether.

16 crows are on
a scarecrow. 7 fly off.
There are 9 crows left.

A chicken lays 4 eggs
one day and 3 eggs the
next day. It lays 7 eggs
altogether.

15 pigs are put into
3 pens. There are
5 pigs in each pen.

- **Write two number stories for a partner to solve.**

Use these signs. $-$ $\times$ $=$

Teachers' note You could introduce number statements using the 'Classroom sorting' activity (see page 5). Different children may give different but correct number statements for the same number story, for example, the first story could be interpreted as 3 x 4 = 12 or 4 + 4 + 4 = 12.

Developing Numeracy
Solving Problems Year 2
© A & C Black

Tell us a story

- **Write a number story for each number statement.**

Example: $20 \div 2 = 10$ 20 children get into 2 teams. There are 10 children in each team.

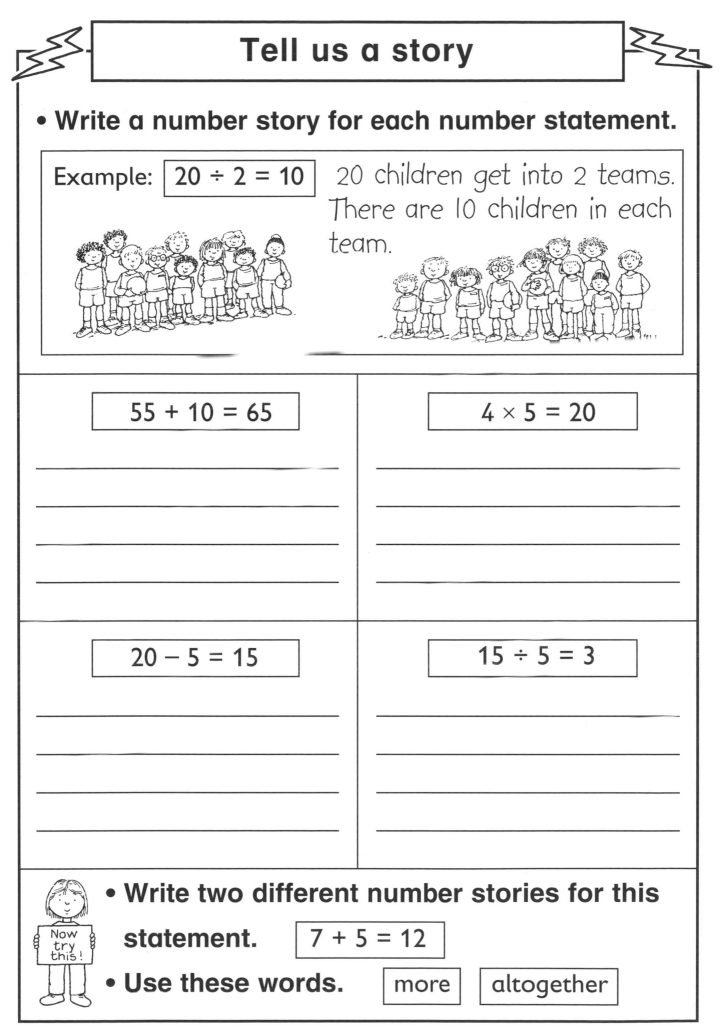

$55 + 10 = 65$

_____
_____
_____
_____

$4 \times 5 = 20$

_____
_____
_____
_____

$20 - 5 = 15$

_____
_____
_____
_____

$15 \div 5 = 3$

_____
_____
_____
_____

Now try this!

- **Write two different number stories for this statement.** $7 + 5 = 12$
- **Use these words.**   more   altogether

Teachers' note This sheet can be used to create missing number statements by masking the instruction, worked example and one number in each statement, for example, □ + 10 = 65. The statements can then be written as number questions, for example: I put 10p in my purse, making 65p altogether. How much did I have in my purse at the start?

**Developing Numeracy
Solving Problems Year 2
© A & C Black**

The maths menace has rubbed out the signs.

• **Fill in the missing signs.**

Use ☐+☐ or ☐−☐.

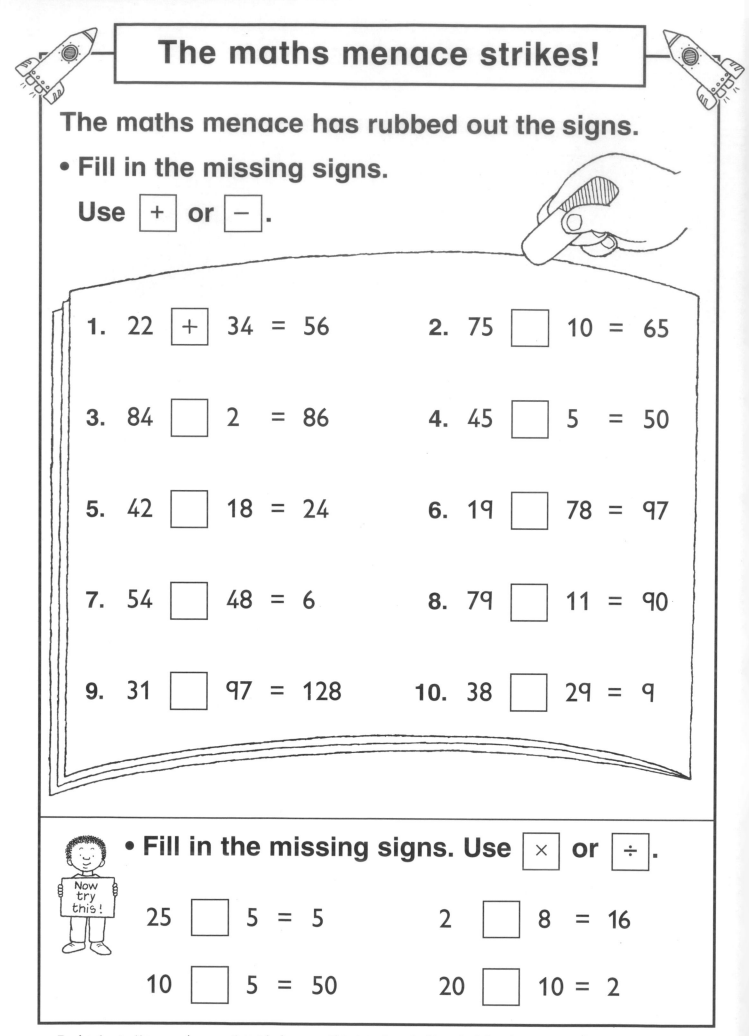

1. 22 [+] 34 = 56

2. 75 ☐ 10 = 65

3. 84 ☐ 2 = 86

4. 45 ☐ 5 = 50

5. 42 ☐ 18 = 24

6. 19 ☐ 78 = 97

7. 54 ☐ 48 = 6

8. 79 ☐ 11 = 90

9. 31 ☐ 97 = 128

10. 38 ☐ 29 = 9

Now try this!

• **Fill in the missing signs. Use** ☐×☐ **or** ☐÷☐ **.**

25 ☐ 5 = 5

2 ☐ 8 = 16

10 ☐ 5 = 50

20 ☐ 10 = 2

Teachers' note Use a number question strip (see page 5) to introduce the idea of missing signs. Encourage the children to realise that, with whole numbers, the largest number in an addition or multiplication statement is the answer, and with subtraction and division, the largest number is the first number.

Developing Numeracy Solving Problems Year 2 © A & C Black

The maths menace has rubbed out the signs.

- **Fill in the missing signs.**

Use $+$, $-$, $\times$ or $\div$.

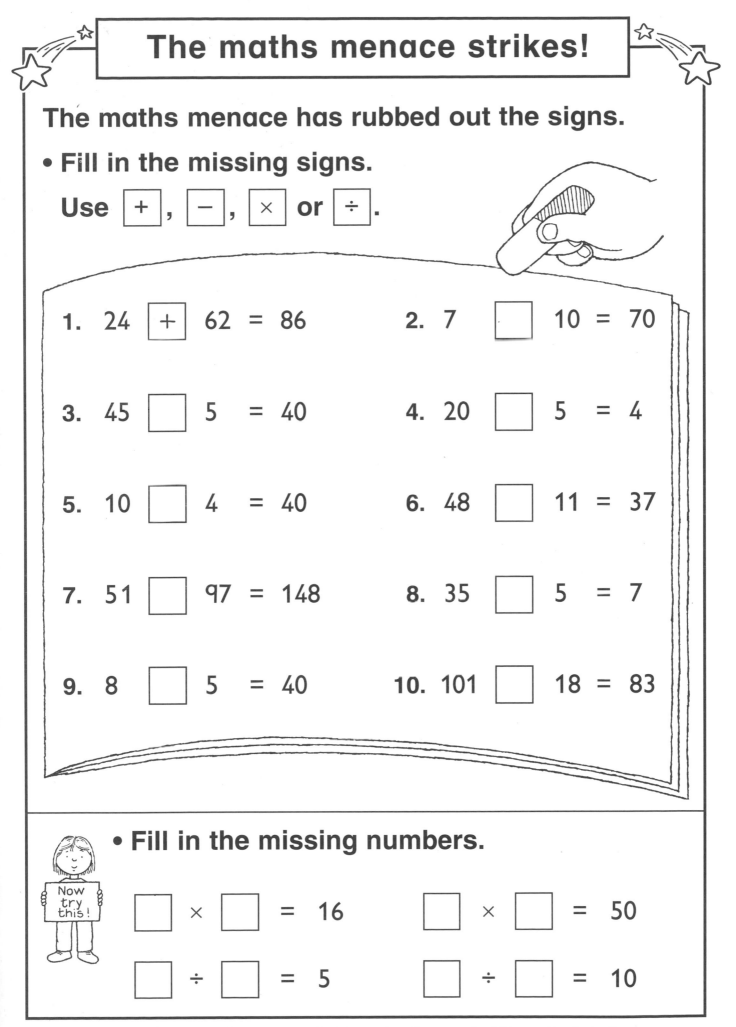

1. 24 $\boxed{+}$ 62 = 86

2. 7 $\boxed{}$ 10 = 70

3. 45 $\boxed{}$ 5 = 40

4. 20 $\boxed{}$ 5 = 4

5. 10 $\boxed{}$ 4 = 40

6. 48 $\boxed{}$ 11 = 37

7. 51 $\boxed{}$ 97 = 148

8. 35 $\boxed{}$ 5 = 7

9. 8 $\boxed{}$ 5 = 40

10. 101 $\boxed{}$ 18 = 83

- **Fill in the missing numbers.**

Now try this!

$\boxed{}$ $\times$ $\boxed{}$ = 16

$\boxed{}$ $\times$ $\boxed{}$ = 50

$\boxed{}$ $\div$ $\boxed{}$ = 5

$\boxed{}$ $\div$ $\boxed{}$ = 10

Teachers' note Introduce the idea of missing signs and missing numbers. Encourage the children to realise that, with whole numbers, the largest number in an addition or multiplication statement is the answer, and with subtraction and division, the largest number is the first number. In the extension activity, discuss why there may be more than one correct solution.

**Developing Numeracy
Solving Problems Year 2
© A & C Black**

How did you do it?

- **Write the answers.**
- **Tick to show how you worked them out.** ✓

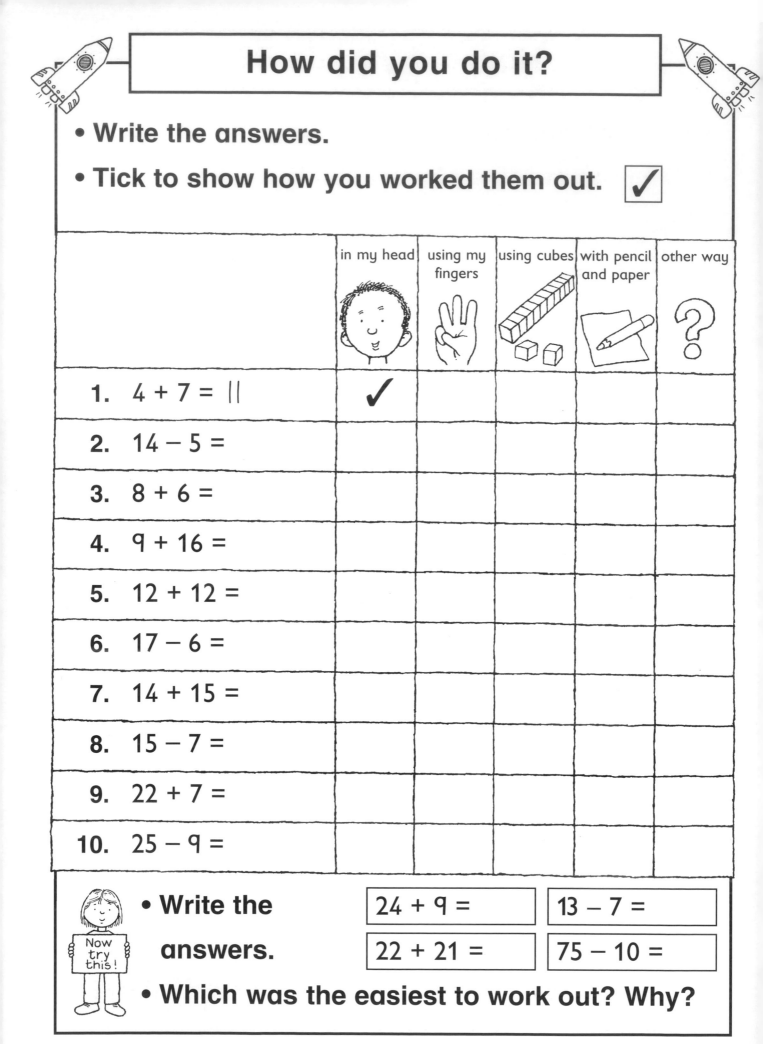

	in my head	using my fingers	using cubes	with pencil and paper	other way
1. $4 + 7 = 11$	✓				
2. $14 - 5 =$					
3. $8 + 6 =$					
4. $9 + 16 =$					
5. $12 + 12 =$					
6. $17 - 6 =$					
7. $14 + 15 =$					
8. $15 - 7 =$					
9. $22 + 7 =$					
10. $25 - 9 =$					

Now try this!

- **Write the answers.**

$24 + 9 =$ $13 - 7 =$

$22 + 21 =$ $75 - 10 =$

- **Which was the easiest to work out? Why?**

Teachers' note Encourage the children to discuss the extension activity in pairs or groups. Why do they think one question is easier than another? Is it because they have memorised the fact or can use their fingers quickly, or do they have a useful strategy for answering questions of this type?

Developing Numeracy Solving Problems Year 2 © A & C Black

How did you do it?

- **Write the answers.**
- **Tick to show how you worked them out.** ✓

	in my head	using my fingers	using cubes	with pencil and paper	other way
1. $4 \times 2 = 8$	✓				
2. $3 \times 4 =$					
3. $6 \times 10 =$					
4. $12 \div 2 =$					
5. $15 \div 3 =$					
6. $6 \times 4 =$					
7. $20 \div 10 =$					
8. $25 \div 5 =$					
9. $6 \times 5 =$					
10. $100 \div 10 =$					

Now try this!

- **Write the answers.**

$18 \div 3 =$ $9 \times 10 =$

$20 \div 5 =$ $5 \times 5 =$

- **Which was the easiest to work out? Why?**

Teachers' note Encourage the children to discuss the extension activity in pairs or groups. Why do they think one question is easier than another? Is it because they have memorised the fact or can use their fingers quickly, or do they have a useful strategy for answering questions of this type?

**Developing Numeracy
Solving Problems Year 2
© A & C Black**

Stamp collecting

You have these stamps in your pocket.

- **Which stamps should you use for each parcel?**

  You can use each stamp only once.

- **Draw the stamps on the parcels.**

You can buy any number of these stamps.

Now try this!

- **Which stamps could you use for this parcel?**

- **Write as many different ways as you can.**

Example:
1p + 1p + 1p + 1p + 20p

Teachers' note This sheet can be used in conjunction with the next to provide differentiation in the main part of the lesson.

Developing Numeracy
Solving Problems Year 2
© A & C Black

Stamp collecting

You can buy any number of these stamps.

1p   2p   5p   10p   20p

- **Write eight different ways you can buy stamps for this parcel.**

$1p + 1p + 1p + 1p + 5p + 10p + 10p$

29p

_____

_____

_____

_____

_____

_____

- **What is the smallest number of stamps you can use?** _____

- **What is the greatest number of stamps you can use?** _____

Now try this!

- **Write as many different ways as you can to buy stamps for this parcel.**

56p

Teachers' note This sheet can be used in conjunction with the previous one to provide differentiation or extension in the main part of the lesson.

Developing Numeracy
Solving Problems Year 2
© A & C Black

All change!

Connor has five coins.

Each coin is less than 20p.

His friend asks him

to change a 20p coin

for some smaller ones.

Sorry, I can't make exactly 20p with any of my coins.

- **Read what Connor says.**

1. Which five coins might Connor have?

   _____ _____ _____ _____ _____

2. Which other five coins might he have? Write as many different answers as you can.

   _____

   _____

   _____

   _____

   _____

   _____

   _____

   _____

Remember that he cannot make exactly 20p with any of his coins.

Now try this!

Connor cannot make exactly 10p either.

- **Which coins do you think he might have?**

Teachers' note Before giving the children this sheet, ensure that they understand what 'changing a coin' means. Discuss situations where exact money is needed, for example, car park ticket machines or slot machines. Ask the children to suggest ways in which coins such as 10p or 20p could be changed for smaller coins.

Developing Numeracy
Solving Problems Year 2
© A & C Black

All change!

Fatima has seven coins.

Each coin is less than 20p.

Her friend asks her

to change a 20p coin

for some smaller ones.

Sorry, I can't make exactly 20p with any of my coins.

• **Read what Fatima says.**

1. Which seven coins might Fatima have?

_____

2. Which other seven coins might she have? Write as many different answers as you can.

_____

_____

_____

_____

_____

_____

_____

Remember that she cannot make exactly 20p with any of her coins.

Now try this!

Fatima <u>can</u> make exactly 15p.

• **Which coins do you think she might have?**

Teachers' note Before giving the children this sheet, ensure that they understand what 'changing a coin' means. Discuss situations where exact money is needed, for example, car park ticket machines or slot machines. Ask the children to suggest ways in which coins such as 10p or 20p could be changed for smaller coins.

Developing Numeracy Solving Problems Year 2 © A & C Black

The cat's whiskers

- **On each whisker, write a question that gives the answer in the cat's mouth.**

  Use these signs. $+$ $-$ $\times$ $\div$ $=$

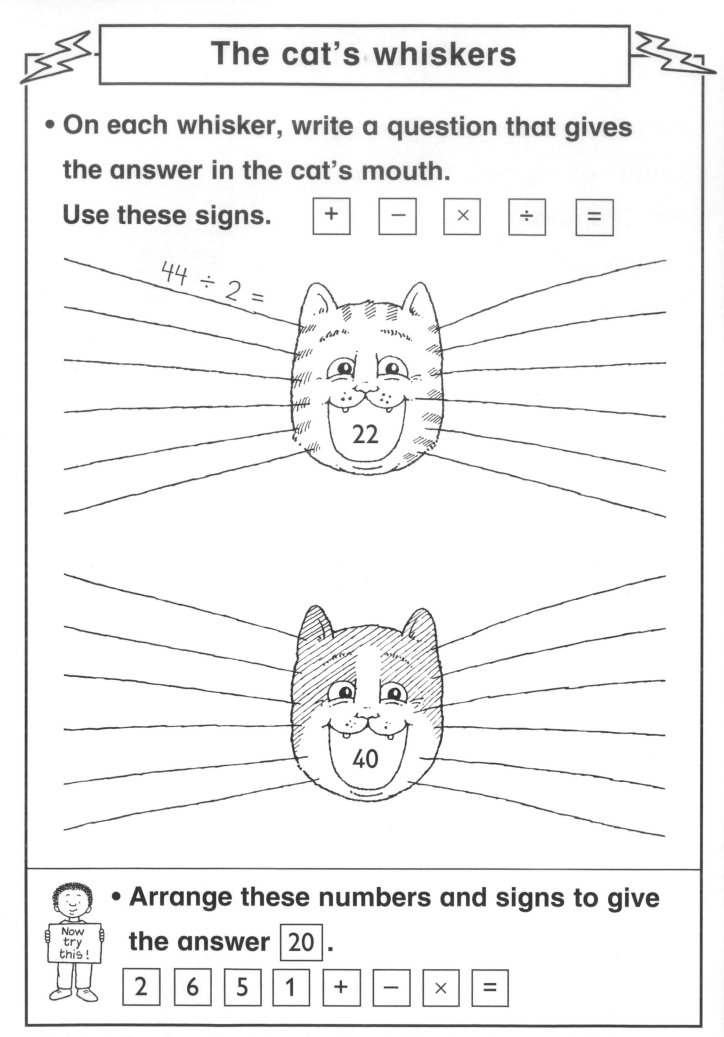

44 ÷ 2 =

22

40

- **Arrange these numbers and signs to give the answer 20 .**

  2 6 5 1 $+$ $-$ $\times$ $=$

Teachers' note The numbers and the worked example could be masked before photocopying to provide a flexible resource. For greater extension, provide 'taboo' numbers and signs, for example 2, 10, +, which the children are not allowed to use.

**Developing Numeracy
Solving Problems Year 2
© A & C Black**

- ## Read how to play 'Crafty counters'.

☆ Put 20 counters in a pile on the table.
☆ Take turns to take away 1, 2 or 3 counters.
☆ Say how many are left each time.
☆ Do not put the counters back in the pile!
☆ The loser is the person who has to pick up the last counter.

Rupa and Tom played the game. Rupa wrote down what happened.

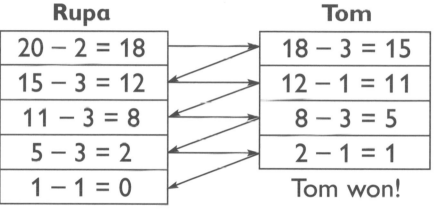

Rupa	Tom
20 − 2 = 18	18 − 3 = 15
15 − 3 = 12	12 − 1 = 11
11 − 3 = 8	8 − 3 = 5
5 − 3 = 2	2 − 1 = 1
1 − 1 = 0	Tom won!

- ## Now play the game with a partner.
- ## Who won?

_____

Name: _____   Name: _____

- ## Play the game more times. Try to find a way of winning each time.

Teachers' note Before the children begin the game, ensure that each child understands the rules and how to record. The resource sheet on page 20 can be cut up and given to children to record further games. See the 'Answers' section for a strategy for winning this game. This can be discussed with the children when they have played and recorded the game many times.

Developing Numeracy
Solving Problems Year 2
© A & C Black

Crafty counters: 2

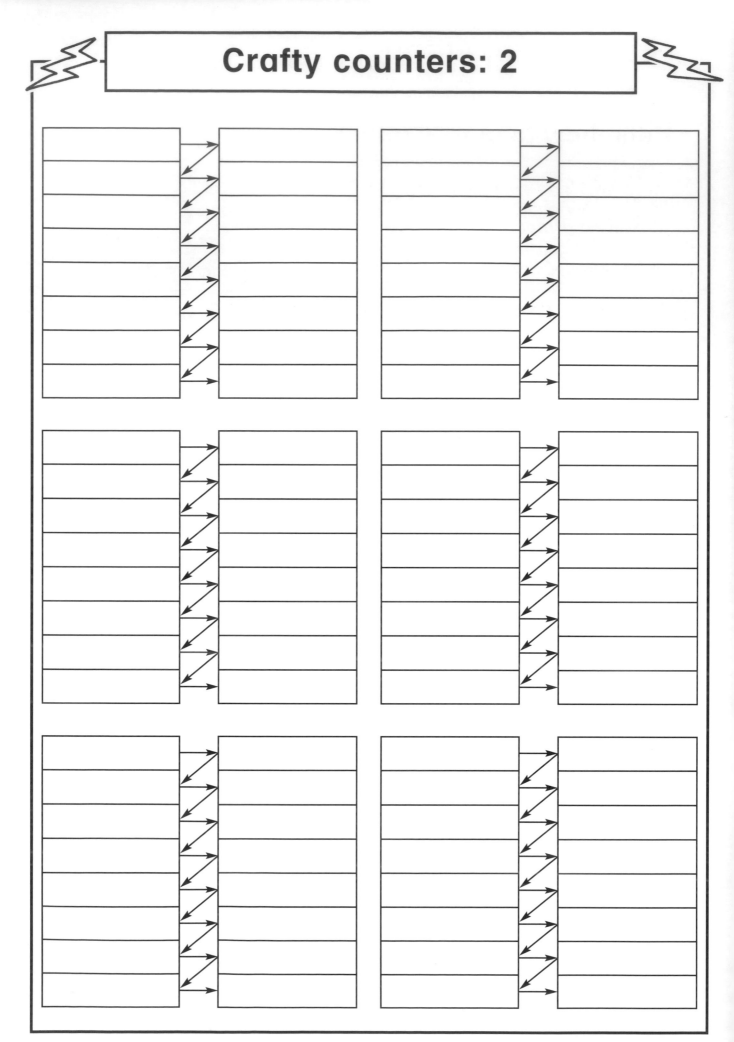

Teachers' note Copies of this resource sheet can be cut up and given to children for recording further games of 'Crafty counters'.

**Developing Numeracy
Solving Problems Year 2**
© **A & C Black**

Quick, quick, cover six

• **Play this game with a partner.**

☆ You will need counters in two colours and three dice.
☆ Take turns to roll the three dice.
☆ Use all three numbers on the dice to make one of the numbers on the grid. Use any of these signs. $+$ $-$ $\times$ $\div$

Example: $3 + 2 \times 4 = 20$ or $2 \times 4 - 3 = 5$

☆ Cover the number on the grid with a counter in your colour.
☆ Write down how you made the number.
☆ The winner is the first player to cover six numbers.

1	2	3	4	5
6	7	8	9	10
11	12	13	14	15
16	17	18	19	20

Teachers' note Before beginning the activity, practise different techniques for adding, subtracting, multiplying or dividing several small numbers (see 'Double, double trouble' on page 5). Discuss the game with the children to ensure that each child understands the rules and how to record. The following sheet can be used to extend this work further.

**Developing Numeracy
Solving Problems Year 2
© A & C Black**

Quick, quick questions

Joe is playing 'Quick, quick, cover six'.
He rolls three dice and makes a
number between 1 and 20, using
the signs $\boxed{+}$, $\boxed{-}$, $\boxed{\times}$ and $\boxed{\div}$.

1	2	3	4	5
6	7	8	9	10
11	12	13	14	15
16	◯	18	19	20

1. Joe rolls $\boxed{5}$ $\boxed{2}$ $\boxed{6}$ and covers the number 17.
How does he make 17? _____

2. Which other numbers between 1 and 20 can Joe
make with $\boxed{5}$ $\boxed{2}$ $\boxed{6}$?

$5 - 2 \times 6 = 18$ _____ _____

_____ _____ _____

_____ _____ _____

3. Which numbers can Joe roll to make 9?
Write as many different ways as you can.

$3 \times 3 \div 1 = 9$ _____

_____ _____

_____ _____

_____ _____

_____ _____

_____ _____

Remember that
dice have only the
numbers 1 to 6.

Now try this!

- **Which numbers can Joe roll to make $\boxed{19}$?**
- **Write as many different ways as you can.**

Teachers' note Before tackling this sheet, the children should play the game on the previous page. The game could be played as a whole class during the mental/oral starter. Encourage the children to find as many different ways as they can and record them on another sheet if necessary. They could explore ways of making other numbers between 1 and 20 in this way.

**Developing Numeracy
Solving Problems Year 2
© A & C Black**

Know your numbers

- **Is the statement** ☐ true ☐ or ☐ false ☐?
- **Colour the correct answer.**
- **Write examples to prove it.**

1. There are exactly four even numbers between 1 and 9.

_2, 4,_   **true**   false

_6, 8_

2. There are exactly four odd numbers between 0 and 10.

_____   true   false

_____

3. There are exactly ten odd numbers between 12 and 22.

_____   true   false

_____

4. There are exactly five multiples of 10 between 8 and 58.

_____   true   false

_____

5. There are exactly five multiples of 5 between 0 and 21.

_____   true   false

_____

6. There are exactly four multiples of 10 between 54 and 81.

_____   true   false

_____

Now try this!

- **If you double any even number the answer is always even.**

true   false

Teachers' note Before beginning this activity, ensure that the children understand the term 'multiple'. You could revise multiples using the 'Counting stick' activity (see page 5). Encourage the children to amend the false statements to make them true.

**Developing Numeracy
Solving Problems Year 2
© A & C Black**

Who is right?

Odd-Bod and Even-Steven can never agree!

- Colour the correct answer.

- Write three examples to prove it.

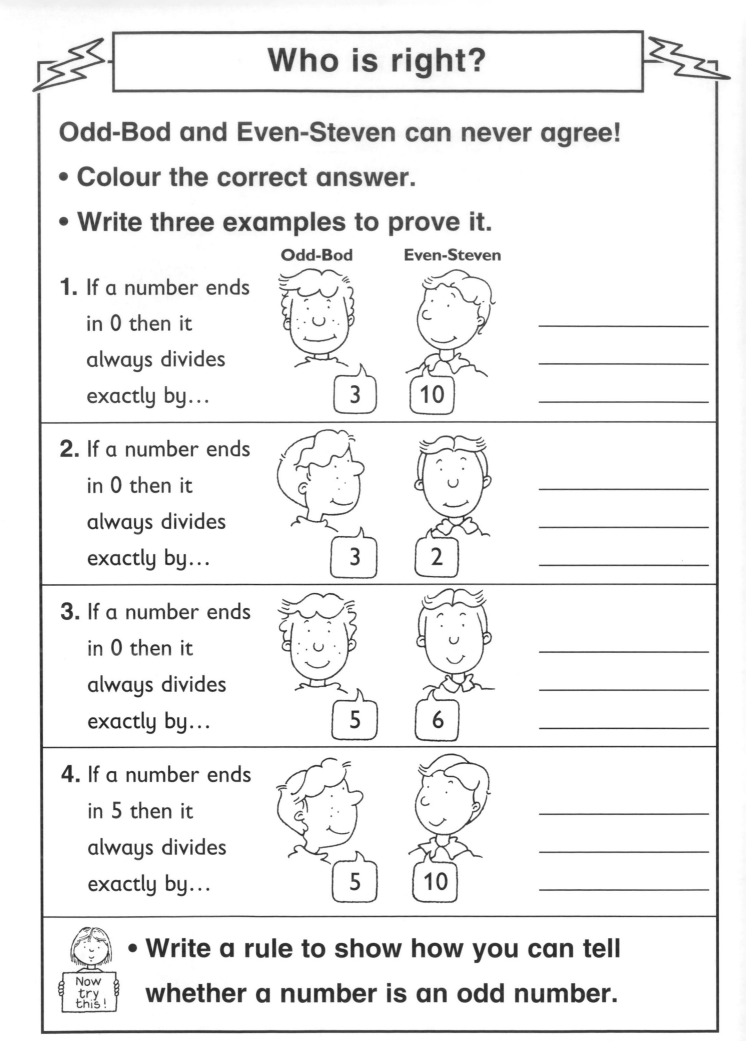

Odd-Bod   **Even-Steven**

1. If a number ends in 0 then it always divides exactly by…   3   10   _____ _____ _____

2. If a number ends in 0 then it always divides exactly by…   3   2   _____ _____ _____

3. If a number ends in 0 then it always divides exactly by…   5   6   _____ _____ _____

4. If a number ends in 5 then it always divides exactly by…   5   10   _____ _____ _____

Now try this!

- **Write a rule to show how you can tell whether a number is an odd number.**

Teachers' note This activity could be introduced to the class as a game. If necessary, revise 'odd' and 'even'. At the end of the lesson, discuss the extension activity with the class and encourage the children to write rules for other numbers, for example, numbers which divide exactly by 2, 5 or 10.

**Developing Numeracy
Solving Problems Year 2
© A & C Black**

Cut-outs: 1

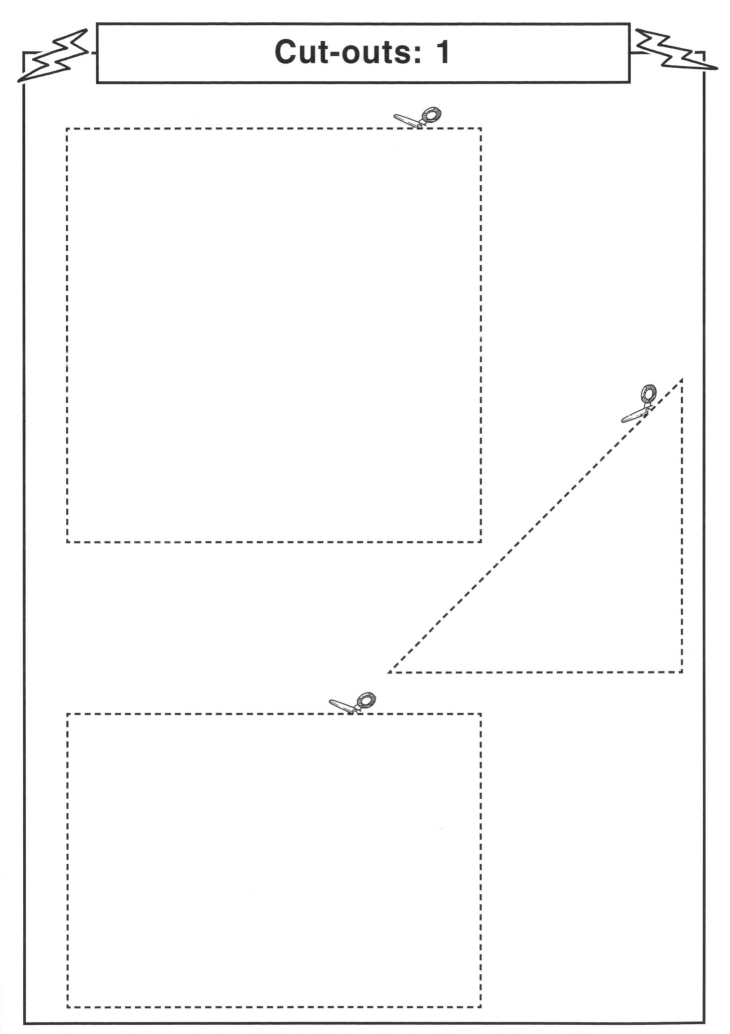

Teachers' note This resource sheet is required for the following activity. The children may find the activity and the cutting out easier if the shapes are coloured in first. Ensure that the children know the names of the shapes; the activity could be introduced using the 'I spy' game on page 5.

Developing Numeracy
Solving Problems Year 2
© A & C Black

Cut-outs: 2

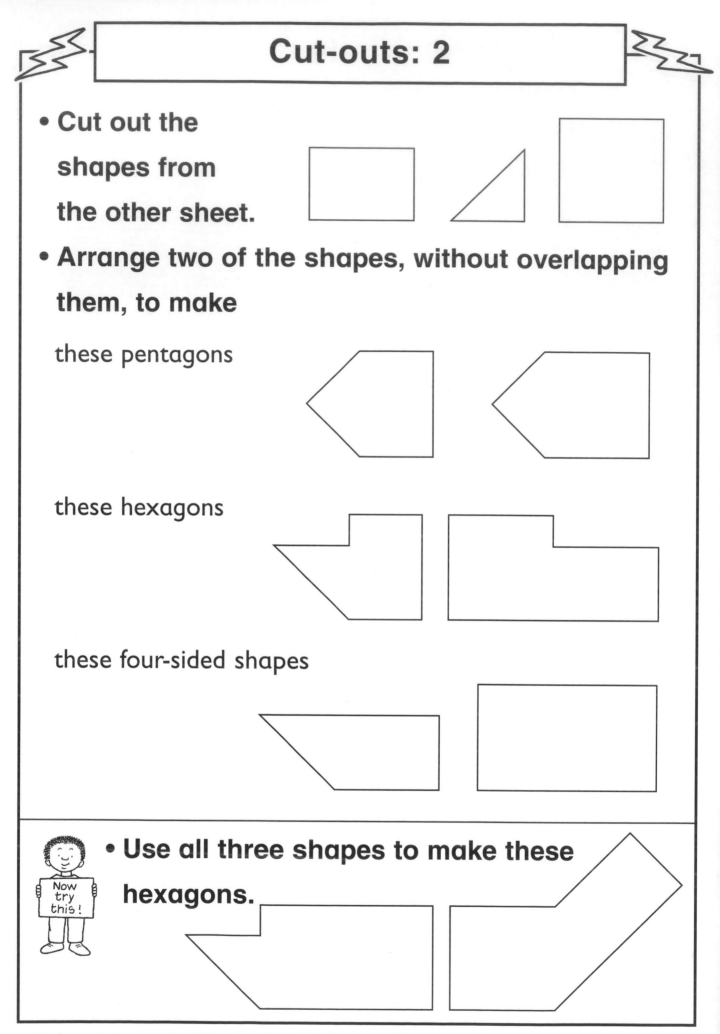

- **Cut out the shapes from the other sheet.**

- **Arrange two of the shapes, without overlapping them, to make**

  these pentagons

  these hexagons

  these four-sided shapes

- **Use all three shapes to make these hexagons.**

Now try this!

Teachers' note Encourage the children to make and describe as many different shapes as they can, using two or three of the shapes. The children can draw the join lines on this sheet to show how they made the shapes.

Developing Numeracy
Solving Problems Year 2
© A & C Black

Pastry shapes

Bertie the Baker has a square of pastry.
The dotted lines show where he might
cut the pastry to make different shapes.

I can make this hexagon.

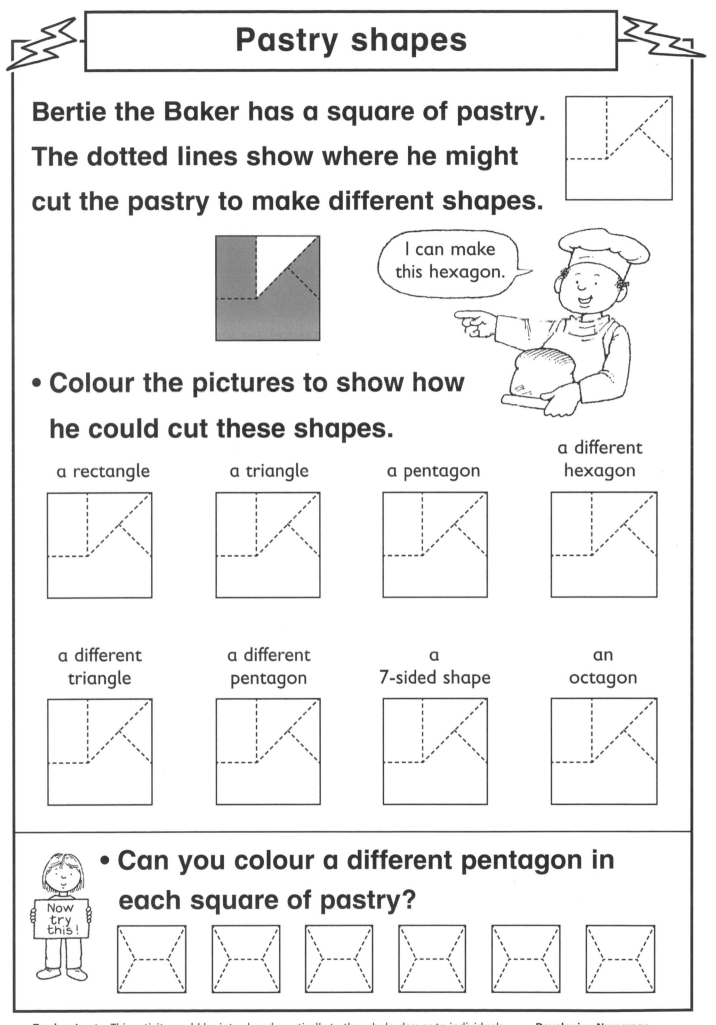

• Colour the pictures to show how
he could cut these shapes.

a rectangle	a triangle	a pentagon	a different hexagon

a different triangle	a different pentagon	a 7-sided shape	an octagon

• Can you colour a different pentagon in
each square of pastry?

Developing Numeracy
Solving Problems Year 2
© A & C Black

Teachers' note This activity could be introduced practically to the whole class or to individuals.
Show the children examples of irregular shapes and remind them that any five-sided shape is a
pentagon, and so on. When completing the sheet, remind the children that they can only colour
shapes that have the edge of the pastry or dotted lines as their sides.

T-shirt teaser

• **Draw five other different ways to arrange these T-shirts in a line.**

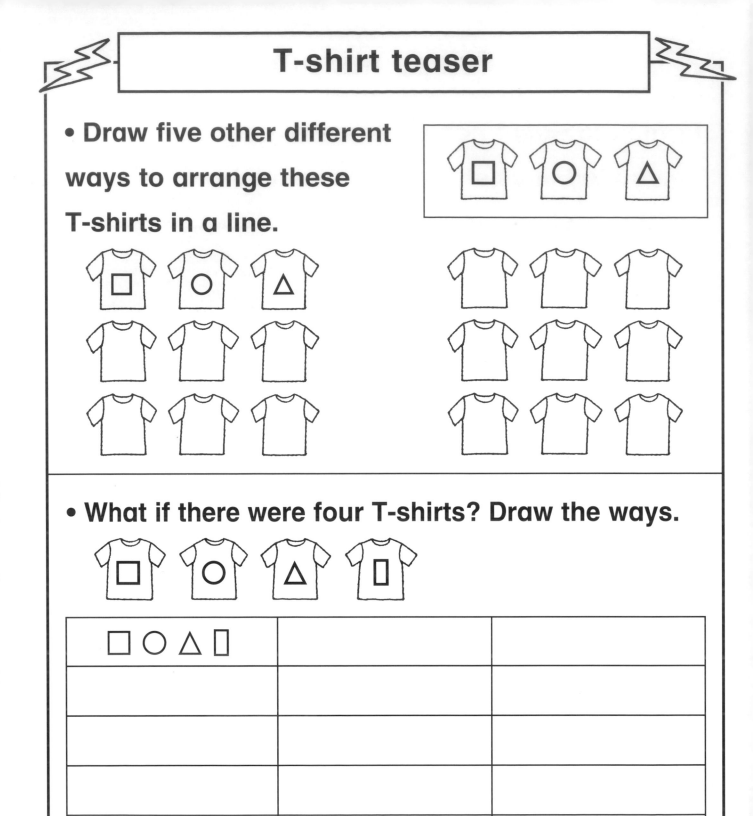

• **What if there were four T-shirts? Draw the ways.**

□ ○ △ ▯		

Teachers' note It may help some children to shade each of the shapes in a different colour. Encourage the children to be systematic, for example, by starting with □ as the first shape and finding as many solutions as they can before moving on to ○ as the first shape, and so on.

Developing Numeracy
Solving Problems Year 2
© A & C Black

Shape mix-up

- **Cut out these shape cards.**

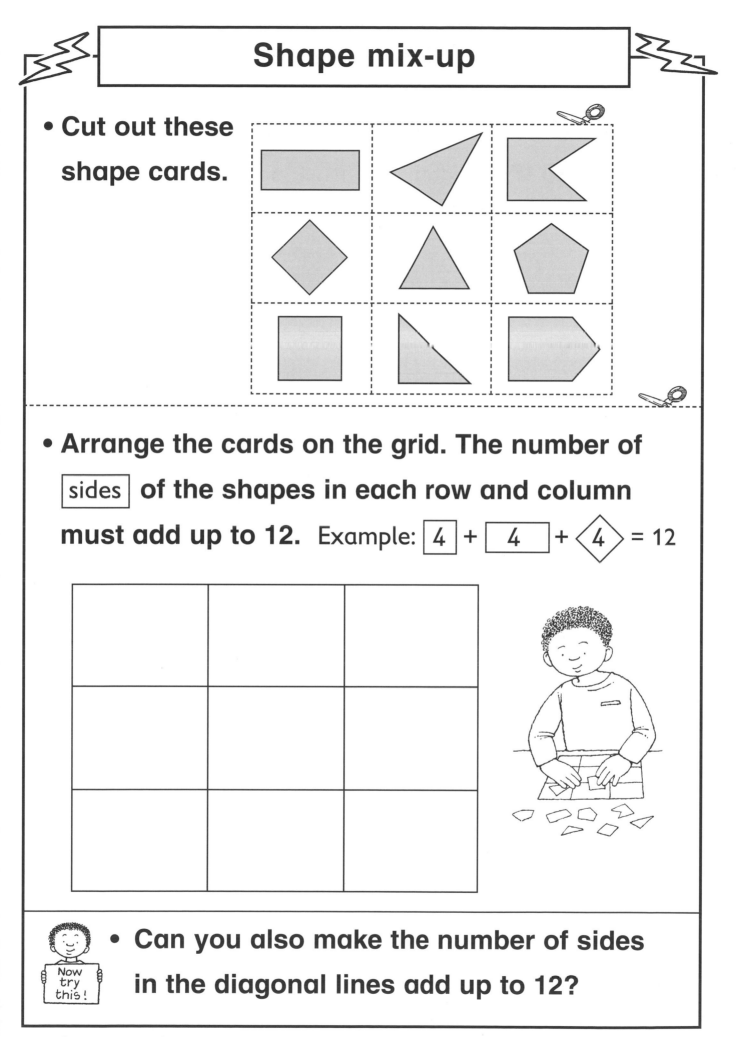

- **Arrange the cards on the grid. The number of** sides **of the shapes in each row and column must add up to 12.** Example: $\boxed{4}$ + $\boxed{4}$ + $\langle 4 \rangle$ = 12

- **Can you also make the number of sides in the diagonal lines add up to 12?**

Now try this!

Teachers' note Ensure that the children understand the terms 'row', 'column' and 'diagonal', and revise the names of the shapes and their properties. It may help some children to count and write the number of sides on each shape before cutting out the cards. When the children have finished, they could stick the cards onto the grid to provide a permanent record.

Developing Numeracy
Solving Problems Year 2
© A & C Black

Maze puzzle

- **Colour all the** triangles **yellow.**
- **Colour all the** rectangles **and** squares **red.**
- **Colour all the** pentagons **blue.**

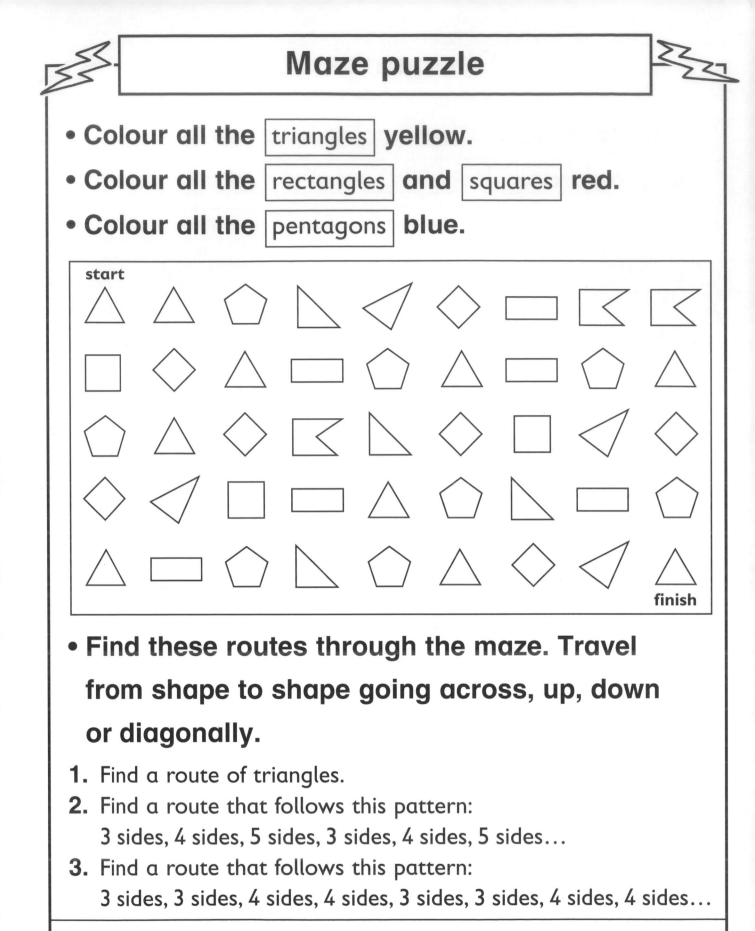

- **Find these routes through the maze. Travel from shape to shape going across, up, down or diagonally.**

1. Find a route of triangles.

2. Find a route that follows this pattern:
3 sides, 4 sides, 5 sides, 3 sides, 4 sides, 5 sides…

3. Find a route that follows this pattern:
3 sides, 3 sides, 4 sides, 4 sides, 3 sides, 3 sides, 4 sides, 4 sides…

- **Draw a maze with 12 shapes.**
- **Challenge a partner to find a route through it.**

Teachers' note Discuss the properties of the 2-D shapes and ensure the children appreciate that any five-sided shape is a pentagon. Revise the terms 'across', 'up', 'down' and 'diagonally'. The more able children could do this activity without colouring the shapes first. Suggest that they draw their routes in pencil first and then draw over them in different colours.

**Developing Numeracy
Solving Problems Year 2
© A & C Black**

True or false?

- **Tick to show whether each statement is** true **or** false.

- **Draw and label some examples to prove this.**

not a square

not a square

a square

All shapes with four straight sides are called squares.

true ☐   false ✔

All shapes with three straight sides are called triangles.

true ☐   false ☐

All shapes with five straight sides are called pentagons.

true ☐   false ☐

All shapes with six straight sides are called octagons.

true ☐   false ☐

Now try this!

- **Write three true statements about shapes for a partner to check.**

Teachers' note Ask the children to test each other's statements to check whether they are true. Remind them of the importance of giving more than one example when checking.

**Developing Numeracy
Solving Problems Year 2
© A & C Black**

I think of a number...

• **What number is each child thinking of?**

1. I think of a number, then add 2. The answer is 18.

2. I think of a number, then add 10. The answer is 10.

3. I think of a number, then take away 5. The answer is 15.

4. I think of a number, then subtract 8. The answer is 9.

5. I think of a number, then halve it. The answer is 7.

6. I think of a number, then halve it. The answer is 12.

7. I think of a number, then double it. The answer is 18.

8. I think of a number, then double it. The answer is 40.

Now try this!

• **Think of a number.**
• **Write a puzzle for a partner to solve.**

Teachers' note Children commonly make mistakes with this type of question by using the inverse operation, for example, giving the answer 20 to the first question. This is because they are using the word 'add' as a trigger rather than understanding the way the question is worded.

Developing Numeracy
Solving Problems Year 2
© A & C Black

I think of a number...

• What number is each child thinking of?

1. I think of a number, then take away 9. The answer is 15.

24

2. I think of a number, then subtract 12. The answer is 20.

3. I think of a number, then halve it. The answer is 15.

4. I think of a number, then halve it. The answer is 14.

5. I think of a number, then double it. The answer is 22.

6. I think of a number, then double it. The answer is 50.

7. I think of a number, then multiply it by 2. The answer is 26.

8. I think of a number, then divide it by 10. The answer is 2.

Now try this!

• Think of a number.
• Write a puzzle for a partner to solve.

Teachers' note Children commonly make mistakes with this type of question by using the inverse operation, for example, giving the answer 6 to the first question. This is because they are using the words 'take away' as a trigger rather than understanding the way the question is worded.

**Developing Numeracy
Solving Problems Year 2
© A & C Black**

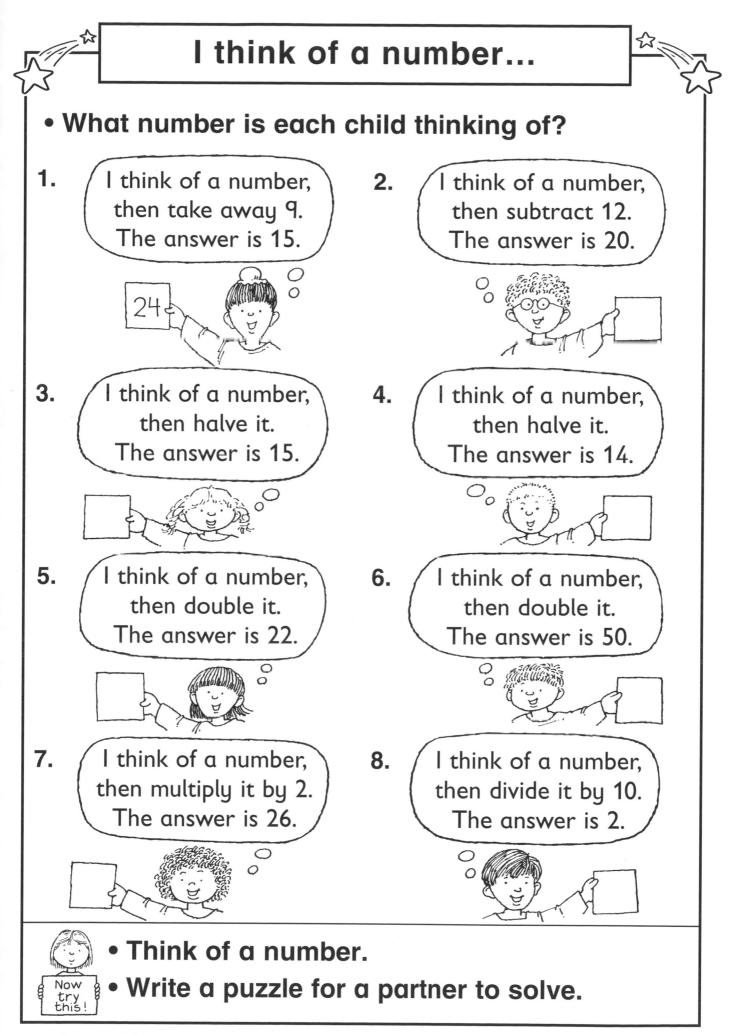

How old?

- **Cut out the cards and put them face down.**
- **With a partner, take turns to answer a card.**
- **Ask your partner to check your answer.**

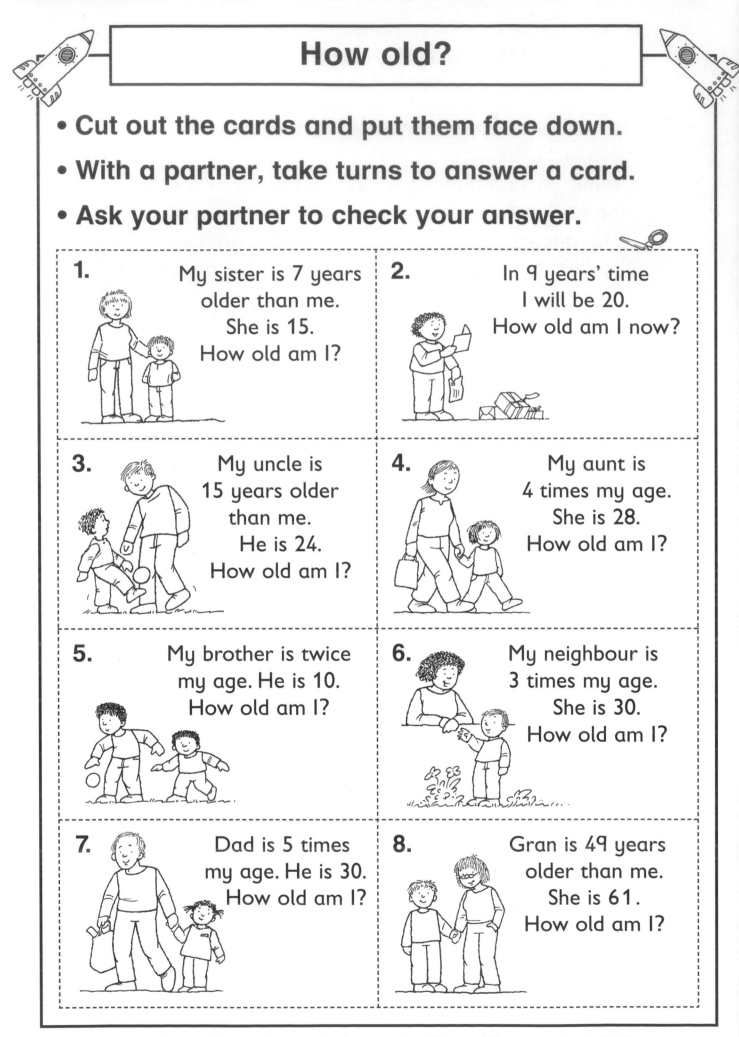

1. My sister is 7 years older than me. She is 15. How old am I?

2. In 9 years' time I will be 20. How old am I now?

3. My uncle is 15 years older than me. He is 24. How old am I?

4. My aunt is 4 times my age. She is 28. How old am I?

5. My brother is twice my age. He is 10. How old am I?

6. My neighbour is 3 times my age. She is 30. How old am I?

7. Dad is 5 times my age. He is 30. How old am I?

8. Gran is 49 years older than me. She is 61. How old am I?

Teachers' note This sheet could be copied onto card for future use. The children could be asked to write the answers on the backs of the cards and arrange them in ascending or descending order.

Developing Numeracy
Solving Problems Year 2
© A & C Black

How old?

- **Cut out the cards and put them face down.**
- **With a partner, take turns to answer a card.**
- **Ask your partner to check your answer.**

1. I am 5. My friend will be twice this age next year. How old is she now?

2. I am 7. My brother will be twice this age next year. How old is he now?

3. I am 6. Dad will be 5 times this age next year. How old is he now?

4. I am 8. Dad was 4 times this age last year. How old is he now?

5. In 4 years' time I will be 12. My sister is half my age now. How old is she?

6. In 8 years' time I will be 20. Mum is 20 years older than me. How old is she now?

7. In 5 years' time I will be 11. Gran is 60 years older than me. How old is she now?

8. 4 years ago I was half the age I am now. Grandad is 10 times my age now. How old is he?

Teachers' note This sheet could be copied onto card for future use. The children could be asked to write the answers on the backs of the cards and arrange them in ascending or descending order. These questions are two-step problems and can be used to provide extension to the question cards on the previous page.

Developing Numeracy
Solving Problems Year 2
© A & C Black

Larry's log-book

• Help Larry to fill in his log-book.

Monday
7 parcels delivered this morning. 8 delivered this afternoon. How many altogether?

Tuesday
20 parcels delivered today. 11 delivered in the morning. How many delivered in the afternoon?

Wednesday
9 parcels delivered this morning. 12 delivered this afternoon. How many parcels in total?

Thursday
Went to 8 houses. Delivered 2 parcels to each house. How many parcels delivered today?

Friday
22 parcels delivered today. 8 delivered in the afternoon. How many delivered in the morning?

Now try this!

Last week, Larry delivered these parcels.

Monday	Tuesday	Wednesday	Thursday	Friday
12	7	9	2	0

• How many did he deliver altogether?

Teachers' note The numbers in these questions can be altered to create more of a challenge or to simplify. The following sheet provides two-step problems in the same context and can be used as an extension or as a differentiated activity in the main part of the lesson.

Developing Numeracy
Solving Problems Year 2
© A & C Black

Larry's log-book

• Help Larry to fill in his log-book.

Monday
7 large parcels and 8 small ones delivered this morning. 4 more delivered this afternoon. How many altogether?

Tuesday
14 small parcels and 6 large ones delivered today. 11 delivered in the morning. How many delivered in the afternoon?

Wednesday and Thursday
24 parcels delivered in total. 15 delivered on Wednesday morning and 6 in the afternoon. How many delivered on Thursday?

Friday
Went to 6 houses. Delivered 5 small parcels to each house. Then delivered 8 large parcels. How many altogether?

Now try this!

Over two weeks, Larry delivered these parcels.

	Monday	Tuesday	Wednesday	Thursday	Friday
Week 1	6	5	9	15	4
Week 2	8	11	0	7	2

• How many did he deliver:

in the first week? ☐   **altogether?** ☐

Teachers' note The numbers in these questions can be altered to create more of a challenge or to simplify. The previous sheet provides one-step problems in the same context and can be used as a differentiated activity in the main part of the lesson.

**Developing Numeracy
Solving Problems Year 2
© A & C Black**

Busy buses

• **Answer these bus questions.**

1.
12 people are on a bus.
5 more get on. How
many people are on
the bus now? __17__

2.
16 people are on a bus.
8 get off. How many
people are on the bus
now? _____

3.
6 people are on a bus.
7 more get on. How
many people are on the
bus now? _____

4.
22 people are on a bus.
13 get off. How many
people are on the bus
now? _____

5.
20 people are on a bus.
6 get on and 8 get off.
How many people are on
the bus now? _____

6.
18 people are on a bus.
11 get on and 15 get off.
How many people are
on the bus now? _____

Now try this!

5 people get on a bus.
There are 11 people
altogether. How many
people were on the bus
at the start? _____

8 people get on a bus
and 4 get off. There are
now 20 people on the
bus. How many people
were on the bus at the
start? _____

Teachers' note Children commonly make mistakes with this type of question by using the
incorrect operation, for example, giving the answer 16 to the first extension question. This is
because they are using the word 'altogether' as a trigger rather than understanding the way the
question is worded. Discuss such trigger words with the children.

Developing Numeracy
Solving Problems Year 2
© A & C Black

Pirates' treasure

- **Work out how many gold coins each pirate has.**
- **Write the number on the chest.**

I have between 20 and 30 coins. If I share them among 10 people I will have 6 coins left.

I have between 10 and 20 coins. If I share them among 10 people I will have 4 coins left.

I have between 30 and 40 coins. If I share them among 10 people I will have 7 coins left.

I have between 10 and 20 coins. If I share them between 2 people I will have 1 coin left. If I share them among 5 people I will have 1 coin left.

I have between 1 and 20 coins. If I share them among 4 people I will have 3 coins left. If I share them among 5 people I will have 4 coins left.

Developing Numeracy
Solving Problems Year 2
© A & C Black

Teachers' note Provide cubes or counters to enable the children to tackle these questions practically and explain to them that 'share' means 'share equally'. Suggest that the children use trial and error, and demonstrate how to do this systematically.

Terrific totals

• **Write the total of the coins in each purse.**

1.
50p
10p 5p

65p

2.
£1
20p 5p

_____

3.
£2
£2 1p

_____

4.
10p
£1
20p 1p

_____

5.
50p
1p 50p

_____

6.
20p 20p
1p 1p 20p

_____

7.
5p
£1 2p
20p 1p

_____

8.
50p £1
5p £2 20p

_____

Now try this!

• **Five coins have a total of** [67p].

None of the coins is a 50p coin.

• **Draw the five coins.**

Teachers' note Further coins could be drawn in the purses to create more complex questions. Provide real or plastic coins to enable the children to work practically.

Developing Numeracy
Solving Problems Year 2
© A & C Black

Join the coins

• **Join the coins to the prices.**

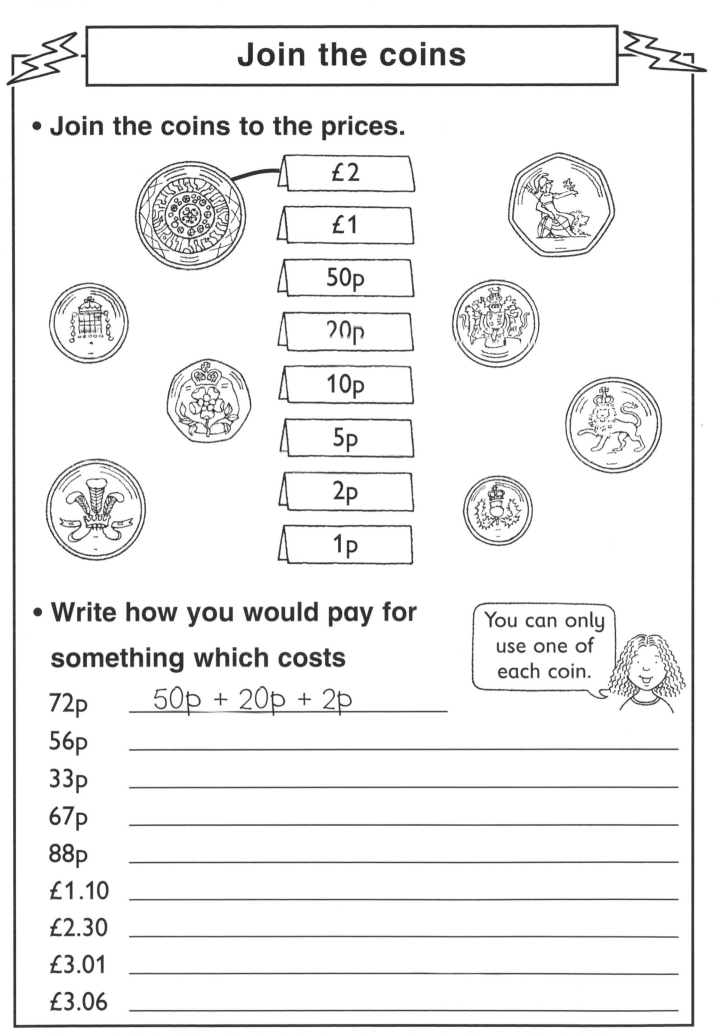

£2

£1

50p

20p

10p

5p

2p

1p

• **Write how you would pay for something which costs**

You can only use one of each coin.

72p   50p + 20p + 2p

56p

33p

67p

88p

£1.10

£2.30

£3.01

£3.06

Teachers' note Provide the children with real or plastic coins to place onto the coin outlines. The coins can be coloured using silver, brown and gold colouring pencils, if available, to reinforce these ideas with the children.

Developing Numeracy
Solving Problems Year 2
© A & C Black

Swap shop

- **You have a** $\boxed{20p}$ **coin. How many**

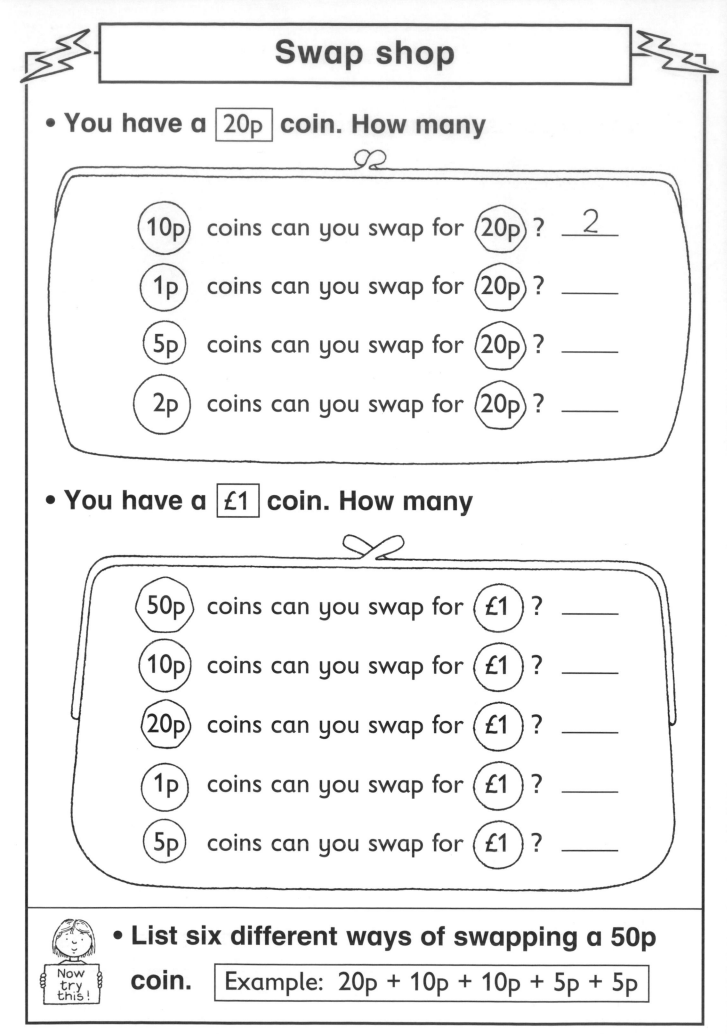

(10p) coins can you swap for (20p) ? ___2___

(1p) coins can you swap for (20p) ? _____

(5p) coins can you swap for (20p) ? _____

(2p) coins can you swap for (20p) ? _____

- **You have a** $\boxed{£1}$ **coin. How many**

(50p) coins can you swap for (£1) ? _____

(10p) coins can you swap for (£1) ? _____

(20p) coins can you swap for (£1) ? _____

(1p) coins can you swap for (£1) ? _____

(5p) coins can you swap for (£1) ? _____

Now try this!

- **List six different ways of swapping a 50p coin.** | Example: 20p + 10p + 10p + 5p + 5p

---

Teachers' note Ensure that the children are familiar with the coins used in real life. They could practise swapping coins of the same value using real or plastic coins. For a further extension activity, the children could explore ways of swapping a £2 coin.

**Developing Numeracy
Solving Problems Year 2**
© A & C Black

Pounds and pence

• **Write these prices using** pounds **and** pence .

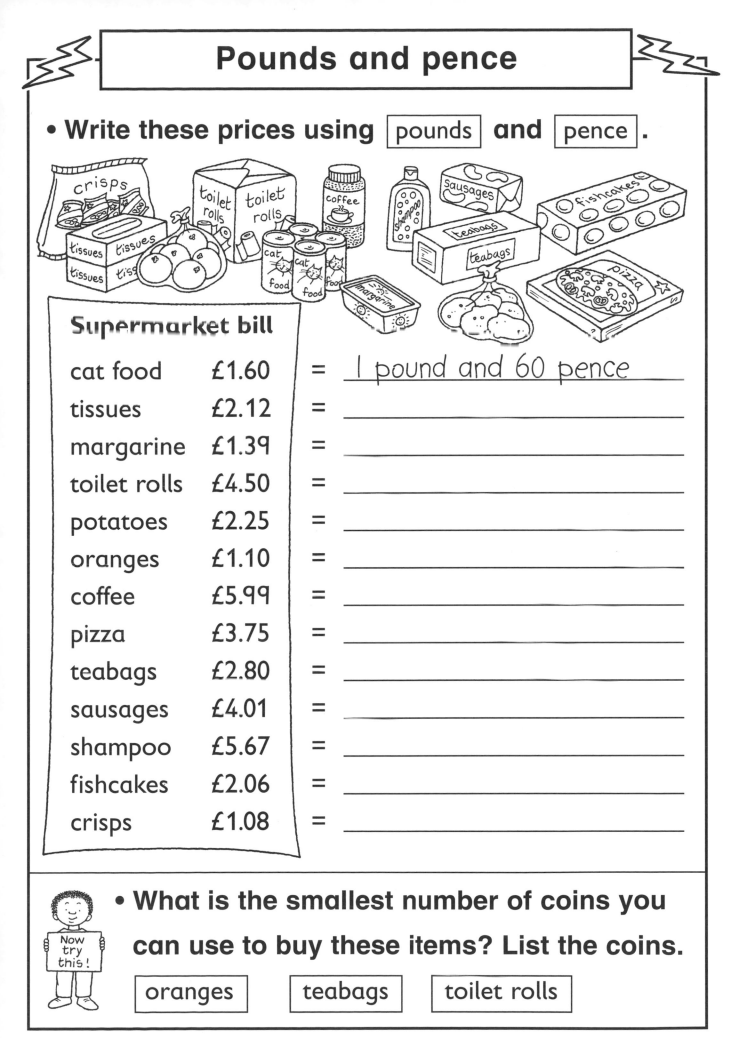

Supermarket bill

cat food	£1.60	=	I pound and 60 pence
tissues	£2.12	=	_____
margarine	£1.39	=	_____
toilet rolls	£4.50	=	_____
potatoes	£2.25	=	_____
oranges	£1.10	=	_____
coffee	£5.99	=	_____
pizza	£3.75	=	_____
teabags	£2.80	=	_____
sausages	£4.01	=	_____
shampoo	£5.67	=	_____
fishcakes	£2.06	=	_____
crisps	£1.08	=	_____

Now try this!

• **What is the smallest number of coins you can use to buy these items? List the coins.**

oranges	teabags	toilet rolls

Teachers' note Ensure that the children are familiar with the coins used in real life. For a further extension activity, the children could explore different ways of paying for these items.

Developing Numeracy
Solving Problems Year 2
© A & C Black

Art attack!

• **Answer the questions.**

6p each

1.

How much will these cost?

12p

2.

You buy these with a 20p coin. What is your change?

_____

3.

You buy these with a 50p coin. What is your change?

_____

4.

How much will these cost?

_____

5.

How can you pay for these exactly with three coins?

_____

6.

You buy these with a £1 coin. What is your change?

_____

Now try this!

Two pencils and a rubber cost 18p **.**

• **How much does a rubber cost?** _____

Teachers' note These questions involve a range of one-step and two-step operations. The activity could be made simpler by changing the price of a pencil, for example to 5p. This sheet can be used in conjunction with the next to provide differentiation in the main part of the lesson.

Art attack!

• **Answer the questions.**

£1 each

Paint 15p each

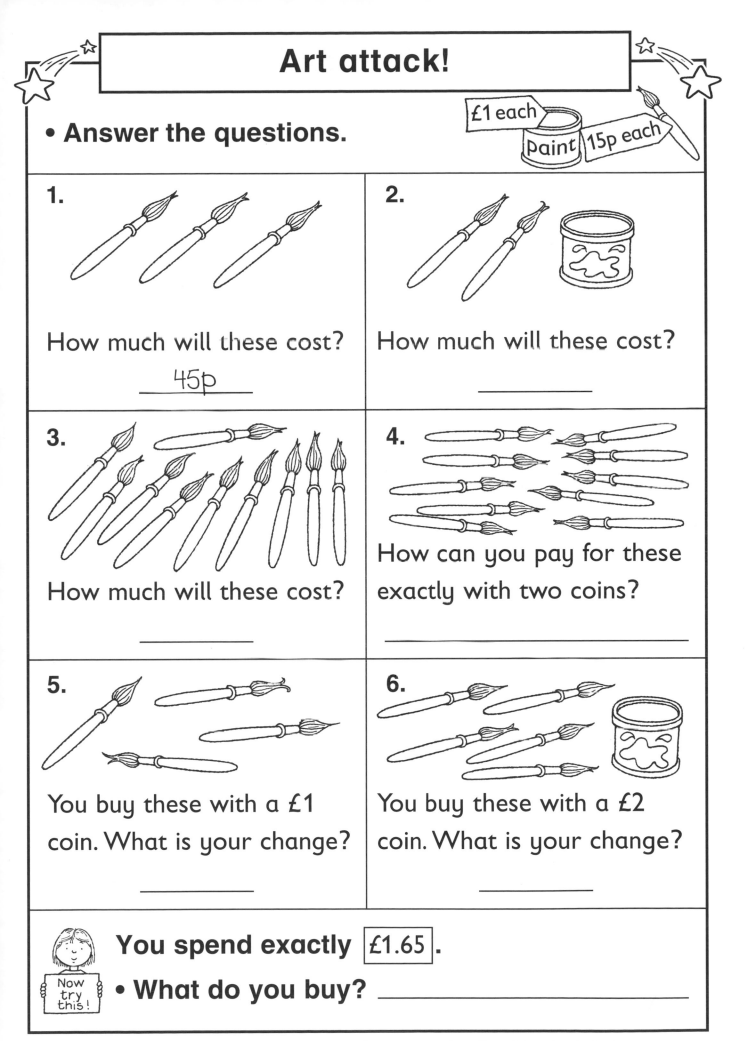

1.

How much will these cost?

_____45p_____

2.

How much will these cost?

_____

3.

How much will these cost?

_____

4.

How can you pay for these exactly with two coins?

_____

5.

You buy these with a £1 coin. What is your change?

_____

6.

You buy these with a £2 coin. What is your change?

_____

Now try this!

You spend exactly £1.65 .

• **What do you buy?** _____

Teachers' note These questions involve a range of one-step and two-step operations. The activity could be made more challenging by changing the price of a paintbrush, for example to 16p. This sheet can be used in conjunction with the previous one to provide differentiation in the main part of the lesson.

Developing Numeracy
Solving Problems Year 2
© A & C Black

Worms, worms, worms

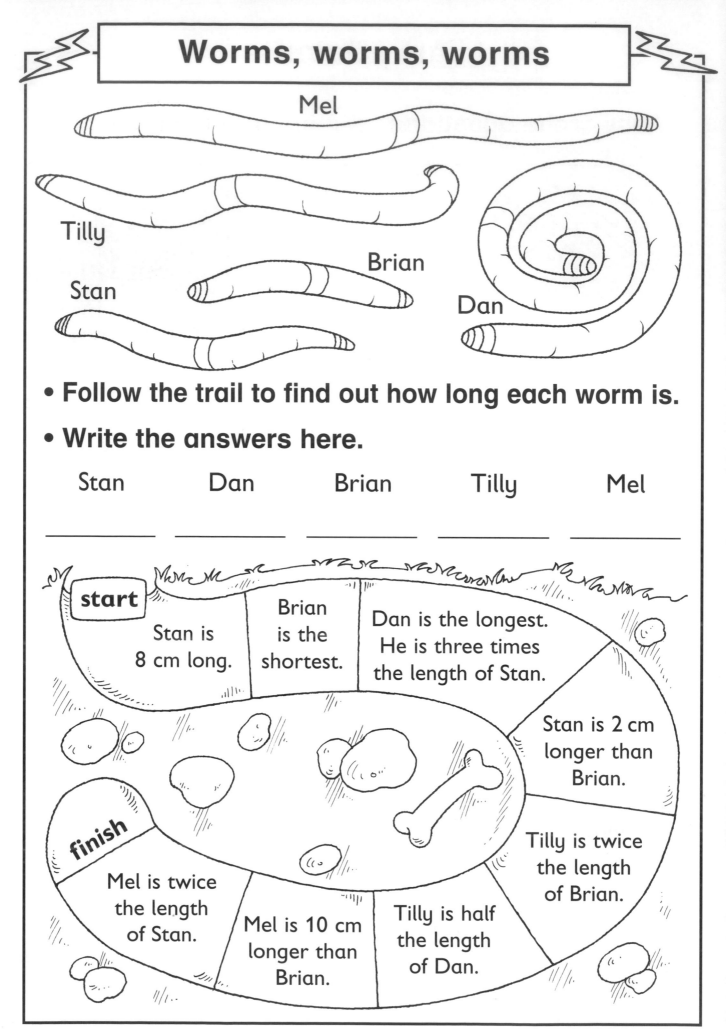

Mel

Tilly

Stan

Brian

Dan

- **Follow the trail to find out how long each worm is.**

- **Write the answers here.**

Stan   Dan   Brian   Tilly   Mel

_____   _____   _____   _____   _____

start

Stan is 8 cm long.

Brian is the shortest.

Dan is the longest. He is three times the length of Stan.

Stan is 2 cm longer than Brian.

Tilly is twice the length of Brian.

Tilly is half the length of Dan.

Mel is 10 cm longer than Brian.

finish

Mel is twice the length of Stan.

Teachers' note Encourage the children to use scrap paper to make jottings if necessary. The original length given can be changed to create more of a challenge or to simplify.

Developing Numeracy
Solving Problems Year 2
© A & C Black

Mighty heights

• **Write the answers to these height questions.**

1. A chicken is 40 cm tall.
A goat is 28 cm taller.
How tall is a goat?

<u>68 cm</u>

2. A chicken is 40 cm tall.
A sheep is twice the height
of a chicken. How tall is
a sheep?

_____

3. A pony is 20 cm taller
than a sheep. How tall
is a pony?

_____

4. A dog is 50 cm tall.
A cat is 15 cm smaller.
How tall is a cat?

_____

5. A duck is half the height of a
goose. A goose is 70 cm tall.
How tall is a duck?

_____

6. A cow measures 1 m 40 cm.
A pig measures 1 m less.
How tall is a pig?

_____

• **A calf is taller than a sheep but smaller than a pony. How tall might a calf be?**

Teachers' note This activity could be introduced practically using children's heights. Remind the children that 'm' stands for 'metres' and 'cm' stands for 'centimetres'. Modelling the situation using a metre stick can help the children to visualise which number operation is required. Encourage them to generate a variety of answers for the extension activity.

**Developing Numeracy
Solving Problems Year 2
© A & C Black**

47

Fruity facts

• **Help Meg to answer Dad's questions.**

1. If a plum weighs 50 g, how much will 3 plums weigh?

150 g

2. How many plums will weigh 300 g?

3. There are 2 kg of apples in a bag. How many kilograms are in 4 bags?

4. How many bags will we need for 12 kg of apples?

5. There are 5 kg of oranges in a box. How many kilograms are in 4 boxes?

6. How many boxes will we need for 25 kg of oranges?

Now try this!

• **If 4 apples weigh** 200 g **, how much does 1 apple weigh?** _____

Teachers' note Remind the children that 'kg' stands for 'kilograms' and 'g' stands for 'grams'. The numbers in the questions could be masked and altered before photocopying to provide more of a challenge or to simplify.

Developing Numeracy Solving Problems Year 2 © A & C Black

Card chain

- **Cut out the cards.**

- **Answer the 'start' card. Find the answer on one of the other cards. Then answer that question, and so on.**

- **Put the cards in a loop on the table.**

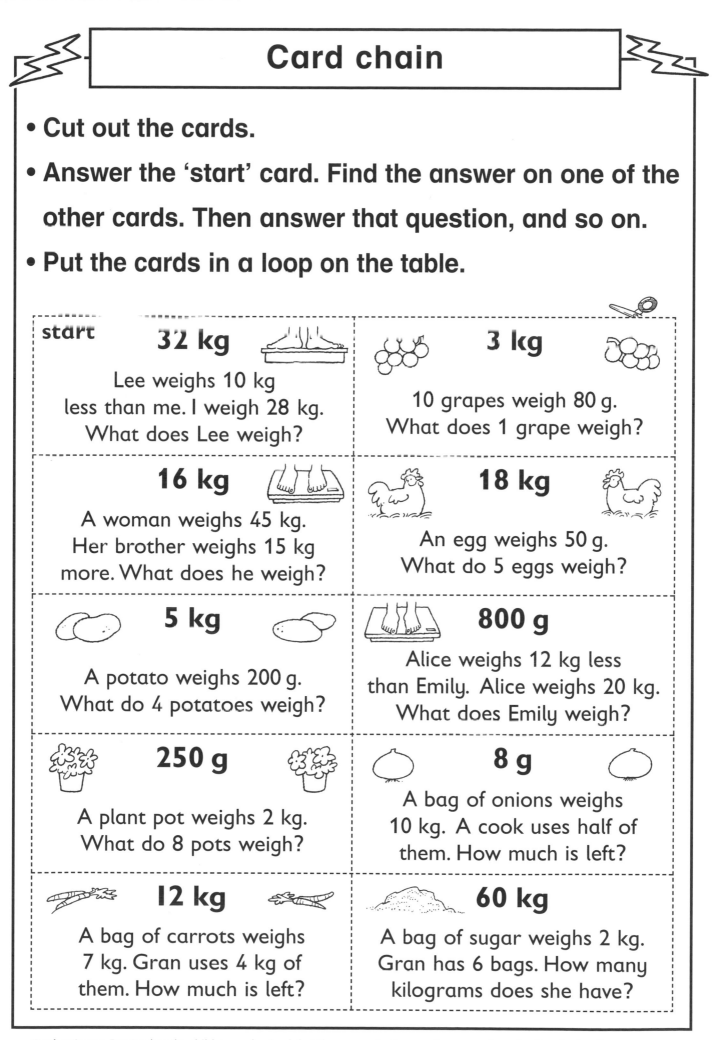

start 32 kg

Lee weighs 10 kg less than me. I weigh 28 kg. What does Lee weigh?

3 kg

10 grapes weigh 80 g. What does 1 grape weigh?

16 kg

A woman weighs 45 kg. Her brother weighs 15 kg more. What does he weigh?

18 kg

An egg weighs 50 g. What do 5 eggs weigh?

5 kg

A potato weighs 200 g. What do 4 potatoes weigh?

800 g

Alice weighs 12 kg less than Emily. Alice weighs 20 kg. What does Emily weigh?

250 g

A plant pot weighs 2 kg. What do 8 pots weigh?

8 g

A bag of onions weighs 10 kg. A cook uses half of them. How much is left?

12 kg

A bag of carrots weighs 7 kg. Gran uses 4 kg of them. How much is left?

60 kg

A bag of sugar weighs 2 kg. Gran has 6 bags. How many kilograms does she have?

Teachers' note Ensure that the children understand that the answer to the question on each card is found on another card and that all the cards form a loop when placed in the correct order. Remind the children that 'kg' stands for 'kilograms' and 'g' stands for 'grams'.

Developing Numeracy Solving Problems Year 2 © A & C Black

Computer colouring

- ## Colour the correct answer.

1.
I have 20 litres
of water. How many
5 litre jugs can I fill?

| 15 | 5 | 4 |

2.
A bucket holds 10 litres.
How much do
6 buckets hold?

| 6 litres | 60 litres | 4 litres |

3.
I fill 7 buckets.
Each bucket holds
10 litres. How much
water do I have?

| 70 litres | 7 litres | 3 litres |

4.
My teapot holds 2 litres.
My kettle holds twice
as much. How much
does my kettle hold?

| 1 litre | 2 litres | 4 litres |

5.
A bath holds 100 litres.
A bucket holds 10 litres.
How many buckets
fill the bath?

| 10 | 90 | 110 |

6.
I have 35 litres of
water. How many
5 litre jugs
can I fill?

| 30 | 6 | 7 |

Now try this!

- ## A 3 litre kettle is half-full of water. How much water is there?

| 1 litre | $\frac{1}{2}$ litre | $1\frac{1}{2}$ litres |

Teachers' note The children will need to think about each question carefully, as many of the incorrect answers look inviting. Discussion between pairs of children is useful here.

**Developing Numeracy
Solving Problems Year 2
© A & C Black**

Fill it up

• **Answer these questions.**

1. This tin holds 5 litres of paint. How much paint is in **3** tins?

15 litres

2. This bottle holds 2 litres of milk. How many bottles do you need to have **6** litres of milk?

3. This bottle holds 2 litres of cola. How much cola is in **9** bottles?

4. A flask holds $1\frac{1}{2}$ litres of tea. Dad fills **2** flasks. How much tea is this?

5. A cook pours oil from a full **12** litre container into some **2** litre bottles. How many bottles can he fill?

6. This bottle holds 3 litres of water. How much water is in **7** bottles?

Teachers' note The children should be encouraged to explain their reasoning to a partner.

**Developing Numeracy
Solving Problems Year 2
© A & C Black**

What time will it be?

• **Colour the clock which shows the correct answer.**

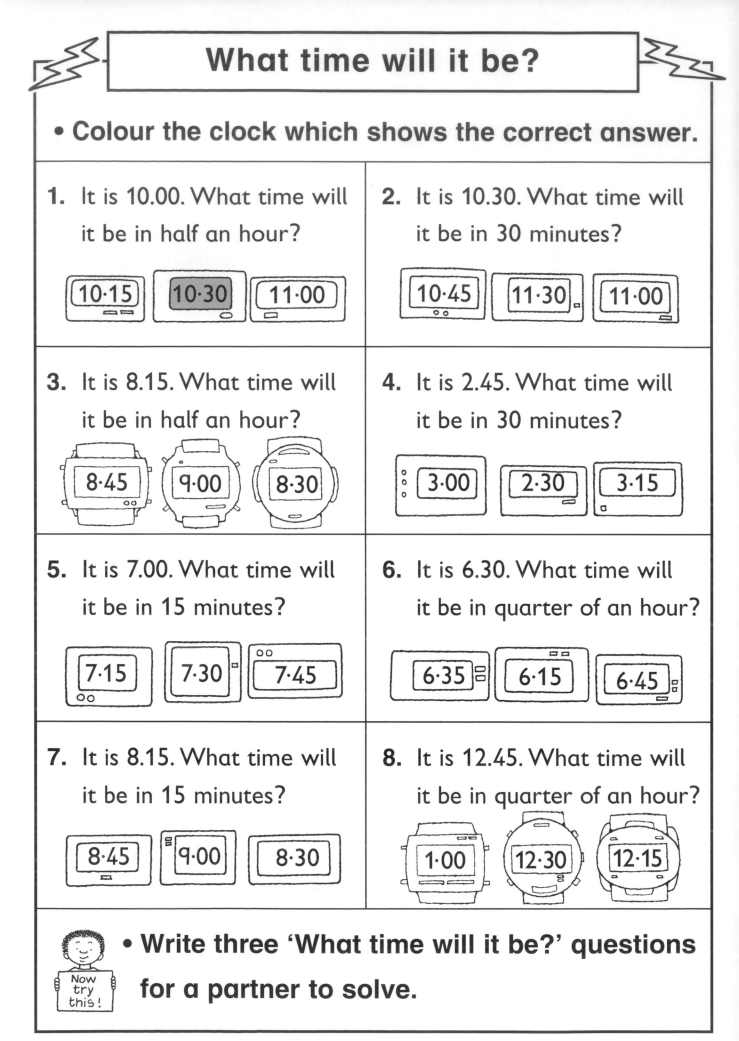

1. It is 10.00. What time will it be in half an hour?

10·15 | 10·30 | 11·00

2. It is 10.30. What time will it be in 30 minutes?

10·45 | 11·30 | 11·00

3. It is 8.15. What time will it be in half an hour?

8·45 | 9·00 | 8·30

4. It is 2.45. What time will it be in 30 minutes?

3·00 | 2·30 | 3·15

5. It is 7.00. What time will it be in 15 minutes?

7·15 | 7·30 | 7·45

6. It is 6.30. What time will it be in quarter of an hour?

6·35 | 6·15 | 6·45

7. It is 8.15. What time will it be in 15 minutes?

8·45 | 9·00 | 8·30

8. It is 12.45. What time will it be in quarter of an hour?

1·00 | 12·30 | 12·15

• **Write three 'What time will it be?' questions for a partner to solve.**

Teachers' note The times could be masked and altered before photocopying to simplify this sheet or to make it more challenging. If desired, provide the children with small clocks to assist them with this activity. The following sheet asks, 'What time was it?', requiring the children to work back from the time given.

Developing Numeracy
Solving Problems Year 2
© A & C Black

What time was it?

• **Colour the clock which shows the correct answer.**

1. It is 10.00. What time was it half an hour ago?

9·45 10·30 9·30

2. It is 7.30. What time was it 30 minutes ago?

7·45 7·00 8·00

3. It is 3.45. What time was it half an hour ago?

3·15 3·00 3·30

4. It is 2.15. What time was it 30 minutes ago?

2·00 1·30 1·45

5. It is 7.30. What time was it 15 minutes ago?

7·15 7·00 7·45

6. It is 8.15. What time was it quarter of an hour ago?

8·05 8·00 8·30

7. It is 11.45. What time was it 15 minutes ago?

11·00 11·30 11·15

8. It is 1.00. What time was it quarter of an hour ago?

1·00 12·30 12·45

• **It is** 12.15 **. What time was it:**

1 hour ago? 30 minutes ago? 15 minutes ago?

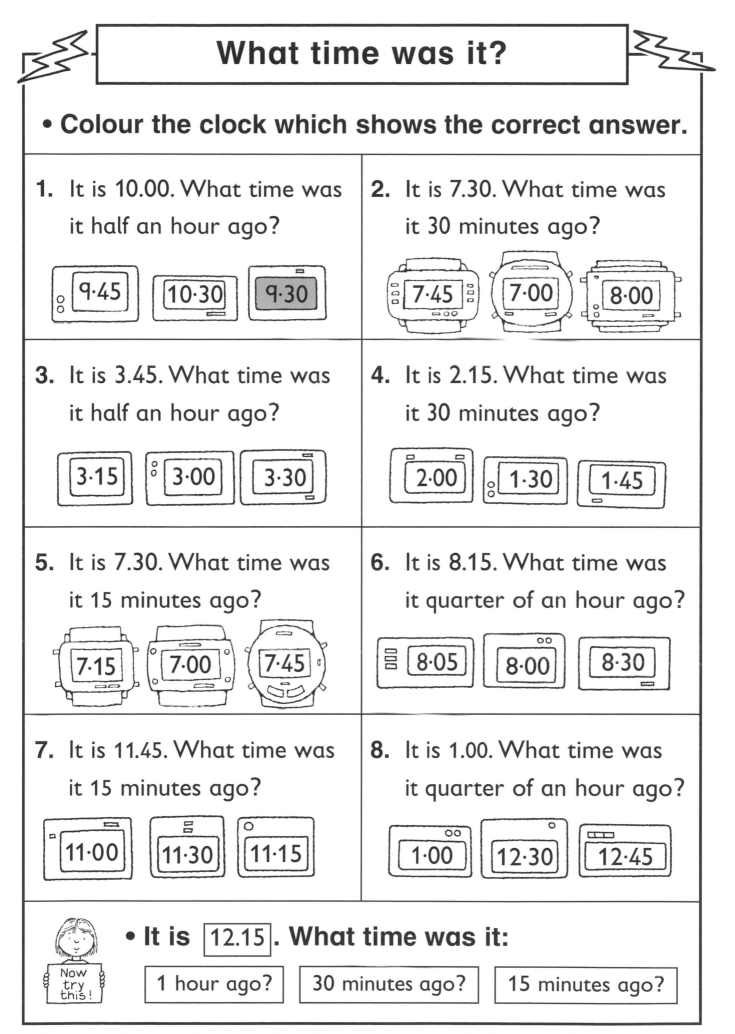

Teachers' note The times could be masked and altered before photocopying to simplify this sheet or to make it more challenging. If desired, provide the children with small clocks to assist them with this activity. The previous sheet asks, 'What time will it be?', requiring the children to work on from the time given.

**Developing Numeracy
Solving Problems Year 2
© A & C Black**

53

Number lists

• **Complete the lists. Write all the numbers you can.**

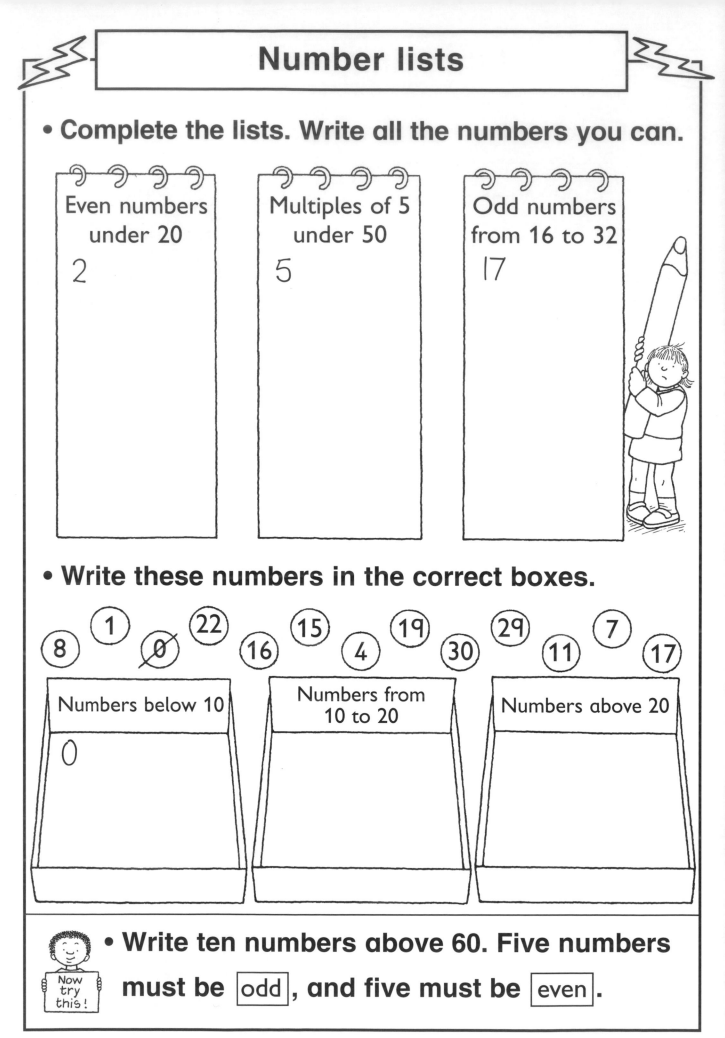

Even numbers under 20

2

Multiples of 5 under 50

5

Odd numbers from 16 to 32

17

• **Write these numbers in the correct boxes.**

8   1   ∅   22   16   15   4   19   30   29   11   7   17

Numbers below 10

0

Numbers from 10 to 20

Numbers above 20

• **Write ten numbers above 60. Five numbers must be** | odd |, **and five must be** | even |.

Now try this!

Teachers' note Remind the children to include all the numbers they can in their lists. Encourage them, where possible, to list numbers in order.

Developing Numeracy Solving Problems Year 2 © A & C Black

All sorts of sweets

• Cut out the cards and sort them into the baskets.

Numbers from 0 to 20	Numbers from 21 to 40	Numbers from 41 to 60

• Which card is left out? _____

54 sweets	70 sweets	10 sweets	12 sweets
35 sweets	16 sweets	25 sweets	8 sweets
47 sweets	55 sweets	27 sweets	34 sweets
36 sweets	45 sweets	24 sweets	19 sweets

Teachers' note Encourage the children to find other ways to sort the cards, for example, odd/even, multiples of 5/not multiples of 5, ascending/descending order.

**Developing Numeracy
Solving Problems Year 2
© A & C Black**

Sorting names

Here are the names of the children in our class.

- ## Sort the names into teams.

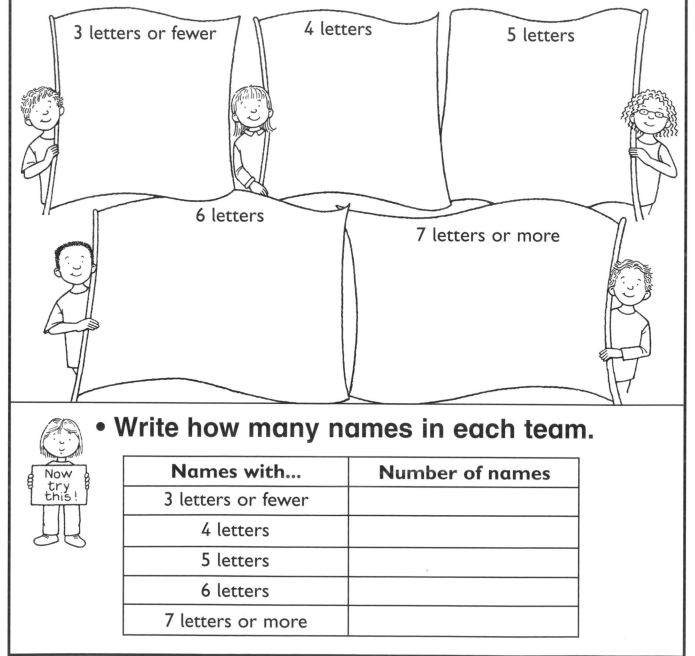

3 letters or fewer

4 letters

5 letters

6 letters

7 letters or more

- ## Write how many names in each team.

Names with...	Number of names
3 letters or fewer	
4 letters	
5 letters	
6 letters	
7 letters or more	

Now try this!

Teachers' note Before photocopying, write the names of the children in the class onto the sheet. Discuss the data collected, asking questions such as, 'What is the most common number of letters in a name?' 'How many names have more than 6 letters?'.

Developing Numeracy Solving Problems Year 2 © A & C Black

Pictogram pies

This pictogram shows the number of pies sold on Monday.

 = I pie

beef	🥧 🥧 🥧
vegetable	🥧
cheese	🥧 🥧 🥧 🥧 🥧
mushroom	
chicken	🥧 🥧

number of pies

1. How many chicken pies were sold? _____

2. Which pie was not sold at all? _____

3. How many meat pies were sold (chicken and beef)? _____

4. Which pie was most popular? _____

5. Which pie only sold two? _____

6. Which pie sold two more than the vegetable pie? _____

7. How many pies were sold altogether? _____

8. Were more meat pies or non-meat pies sold? _____

• Draw a pictogram to show how many pies might be sold on Tuesday.

Now try this!

Teachers' note Draw the children's attention to the key, showing that one pie symbol represents one pie sold. To provide further extension work, change the key before photocopying to show one pie symbol representing two pies. The same questions can be answered.

Developing Numeracy
Solving Problems Year 2
© A & C Black

Pictogram pizzas

This chart shows the number of pizzas sold on Friday.

Pizzas	Number sold
cheese and tomato	2
tuna and sweetcorn	4
pepperoni	6
ham and pineapple	1
mega-pizza	5

• Complete the pictogram to show this information.

 = 1 pizza

cheese and tomato					
tuna and sweetcorn					
pepperoni					
ham and pineapple					
mega-pizza					

number of pizzas

1. How many tuna and sweetcorn pizzas were sold? _____

2. Which pizza was most popular? _____

3. Which pizza sold two more than

   the tuna and sweetcorn? _____

4. How many pizzas were sold altogether? _____

Now try this!

• Draw a pictogram to show how many pizzas might be sold on Saturday.

Teachers' note Draw the children's attention to the key, showing that one pizza symbol represents one pizza sold. To provide further extension work, change the key before photocopying to show one pizza symbol representing two pizzas (a half pizza can be drawn to represent one pizza in this case). The same questions can be answered.

Developing Numeracy
Solving Problems Year 2
© A & C Black

Roadblock

This graph shows the colours of the cars parked in Ahmed's street.

• **Colour the blocks.**

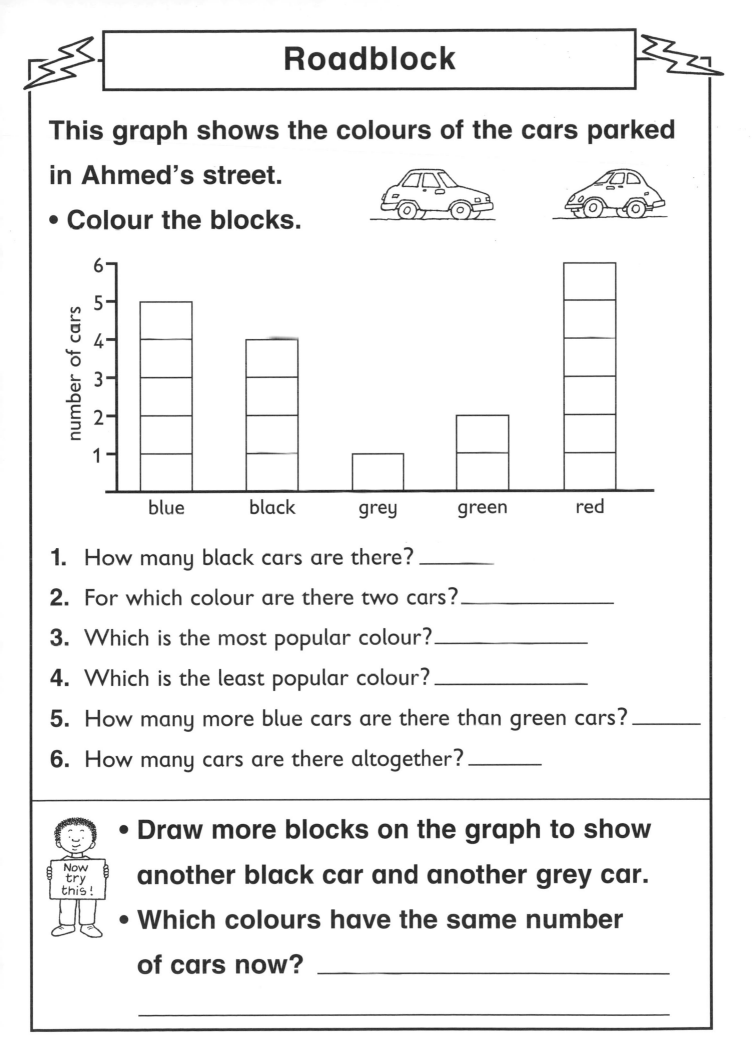

1. How many black cars are there? _____

2. For which colour are there two cars? _____

3. Which is the most popular colour? _____

4. Which is the least popular colour? _____

5. How many more blue cars are there than green cars? _____

6. How many cars are there altogether? _____

• **Draw more blocks on the graph to show another black car and another grey car.**

• **Which colours have the same number of cars now?** _____

_____

Teachers' note Further questions can be asked about this graph, such as, 'Were there any pink cars?' 'Who might find the information on this graph useful?' 'Do you think the graph might be the same for your street?' 'Could we draw a similar graph for the cars in our street?'.

**Developing Numeracy
Solving Problems Year 2
© A & C Black**

Block graph

Here are family names of some children in our class.

[blank box]

• **Write the names on the chart.**

Number of letters	Family names	Total
3 letters or fewer		
4 letters		
5 letters		
6 letters		
7 letters or more		

• Complete the block graph to show this information.

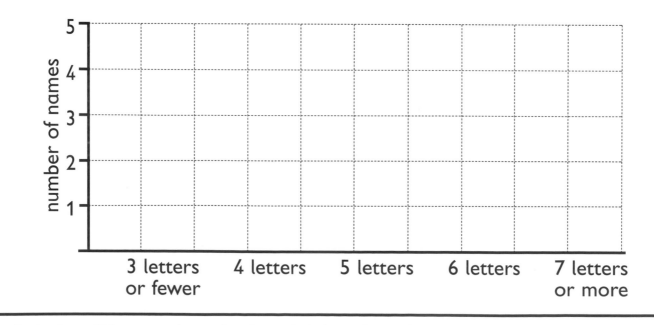

number of names

3 letters or fewer   4 letters   5 letters   6 letters   7 letters or more

Teachers' note Fill in an appropriate number of names in the box at the top of the sheet for the children to work with (depending on their ability). Ensure that the children understand the meaning of 'family name'. Other sorts of information could be used to create similar block graphs, for example pets, hair colour, method of travelling to school.

**Developing Numeracy
Solving Problems Year 2
© A & C Black**

Let's investigate!

• **Which flavours of crisps do children in our class like best? Fill in the chart.**

Flavour	Names of children	Total
salt and vinegar		
cheese and onion		
chicken		
prawn cocktail		
other flavour		

• **Draw a pictogram or a block graph to show this information.**

Teachers' note Encourage the children to discuss how best to complete the survey, for example, call out a flavour and the children vote with their hands. Alternatively, names can be pre-written on the chart and the children can draw a pictogram or block graph to show this information. For block graphs, provide the children with cubes or squares to draw around.

**Developing Numeracy
Solving Problems Year 2
© A & C Black**

Shoe survey

- **Which shoe sizes do children in our class have? Fill in the chart.**

Shoe size	Names of children	Total
size 11 or smaller		
size 12		
size 13		
size 1		
size 2 or larger		

- **Draw a pictogram or a block graph to show this information.**

Teachers' note Encourage the children to discuss how best to complete the survey, for example, call out a size and the children vote with their hands or by holding up digit cards to show their size. Alternatively, names can be pre-written on the chart. For block graphs, provide the children with cubes or squares to draw around.

**Developing Numeracy
Solving Problems Year 2
© A & C Black**

Answers

p 6
Now try this!
10 + 8 − 2 = 16 **or** 10 + 4 + 2 = 16

p 7
1. 22   **2.** 23   **3.** 85   **4.** 18   **5.** 27   **6.** 22
Now try this!
26   4

p 8
3 × 4 = 12   16 − 7 = 9
4 + 3 = 7   15 ÷ 3 = 5

p 10
1. +   **2.** −   **3.** +   **4.** +   **5.** −
6. +   **7.** −   **8.** +   **9.** +   **10.** −
Now try this!
÷   ×
×   ÷

p 11
1. +   **2.** ×   **3.** −   **4.** ÷   **5.** ×
6. −   **7.** +   **8.** ÷   **9.** ×   **10.** −

p 12
1. 11   **2.** 9   **3.** 14   **4.** 25   **5.** 24
6. 11   **7.** 29   **8.** 8   **9.** 29   **10.** 16
Now try this!
24 + 9 = 33   13 − 7 = 6
22 + 21 = 43   75 − 10 = 65

p 13
1. 8   **2.** 12   **3.** 60   **4.** 6   **5.** 5
6. 24   **7.** 2   **8.** 5   **9.** 30   **10.** 10
Now try this!
18 ÷ 3 = 6   9 × 10 = 90
20 ÷ 5 = 4   5 × 5 = 25

p 14
20p = 12p + 8p   16p = 15p + 1p   7p = 5p + 2p
Now try this!
Check the different ways of making 24p.

p 15
Check the different ways of making 29p.
Smallest number = 4 stamps: 20p + 5p + 2p + 2p
Greatest number = 29 stamps: 1p + 1p + 1p...

p 16
There are many solutions, e.g.
1p + 1p + 1p + 1p + 1p   10p + 2p + 2p + 2p + 1p
2p + 1p + 1p + 1p + 1p   10p + 2p + 2p + 2p + 2p
2p + 2p + 1p + 1p + 1p   10p + 5p + 1p + 1p + 1p
2p + 2p + 2p + 1p + 1p   10p + 5p + 2p + 1p + 1p
2p + 2p + 2p + 2p + 1p   10p + 5p + 2p + 2p + 2p
2p + 2p + 2p + 2p + 2p   5p + 2p + 1p + 1p + 1p
5p + 1p + 1p + 1p + 1p   5p + 2p + 2p + 1p + 1p
5p + 5p + 1p + 1p + 1p   5p + 2p + 2p + 2p + 1p
5p + 5p + 5p + 1p + 1p   **5p + 2p + 2p + 2p + 2p**
10p + 1p + 1p + 1p + 1p   5p + 5p + 2p + 1p + 1p
10p + 2p + 1p + 1p + 1p   5p + 5p + 2p + 2p + 1p
10p + 2p + 2p + 1p + 1p   5p + 5p + 5p + 2p + 2p
Those in **bold** are the coins referred to in the 'Now try this!' task.

p 17
There are many solutions, e.g.
1p + 1p + 1p + 1p + 1p + 1p + 1p   **5p + 5p + 2p + 1p + 1p + 1p + 1p**
2p + 1p + 1p + 1p + 1p + 1p + 1p   **5p + 5p + 2p + 2p + 1p + 1p + 1p**
2p + 2p + 1p + 1p + 1p + 1p + 1p   **5p + 5p + 2p + 2p + 2p + 1p + 1p**
2p + 2p + 2p + 1p + 1p + 1p + 1p   **5p + 5p + 2p + 2p + 2p + 2p + 1p**
2p + 2p + 2p + 2p + 1p + 1p + 1p   5p + 1p + 1p + 1p + 1p + 1p + 1p
2p + 2p + 2p + 2p + 2p + 1p + 1p   **5p + 5p + 1p + 1p + 1p + 1p + 1p**
5p + 2p + 1p + 1p + 1p + 1p + 1p   **5p + 5p + 5p + 1p + 1p + 1p + 1p**
5p + 2p + 2p + 1p + 1p + 1p + 1p   10p + 1p + 1p + 1p + 1p + 1p + 1p
5p + 2p + 2p + 2p + 1p + 1p + 1p   10p + 2p + 1p + 1p + 1p + 1p + 1p
5p + 2p + 2p + 2p + 2p + 1p + 1p   10p + 2p + 2p + 1p + 1p + 1p + 1p
5p + 2p + 2p + 2p + 2p + 2p + 1p   10p + 2p + 2p + 2p + 1p + 1p + 1p
5p + 2p + 2p + 2p + 2p + 2p + 2p
Those in **bold** are the coins referred to in the 'Now try this!' task.

p 18
Now try this!
6 + 5 − 1 × 2 = 20

p 19
There is a strategy for winning the game. From the start of the game, at each turn, try to leave 17, 13, 9 or 5 counters on the table. This will ensure the other player is the one to pick up the last counter.

p 22
1. 6 × 2 + 5 = 17
2. Solutions include:
5 + 2 − 6 = 1   (6 − 5) × 2 − 2 **or** 5 − (6 ÷ 2) = 2
6 − 5 + 2 = 3   5 × 2 − 6 = 4   6 × 2 − 5 = 7
6 ÷ 2 + 5 = 8   5 − 2 + 6 = 9   6 + 5 + 2 = 13
6 × 5 ÷ 2 = 15   5 × 2 + 6 = 16   6 × 2 + 5 = 17
(5 − 2) × 6 = 18
3. Any solutions such as those below, using numbers 1 to 6 and equalling 9:
1 + 2 + 6   2 + 2 + 5   3 + 2 + 4   3 + 3 + 3   4 + 4 + 1
5 + 3 + 1   5 + 5 − 1   6 + 5 − 2   6 + 6 − 3   (4 + 5) × 1
(3 + 6) × 1   2 × 4 + 1   2 × 3 + 3   2 × 2 + 5   2 × 5 − 1
2 × 6 − 3   3 × 3 × 1
Now try this!
Any solutions such as those below, using numbers 1 to 6 and equalling 19:
3 × 5 + 4   3 × 6 + 1   5 × 4 − 1
6 × 4 − 5   5 × 5 − 6   4 × 4 + 3

p 23
1. True   **2.** False. There are 5.   **3.** False. There are 5.
4. True   **5.** False. There are 4.   **6.** False. There are 3.
Now try this!
True

p 24
1. 10   **2.** 2   **3.** 5   **4.** 5

p 26
pentagons   hexagons

four-sided shapes   **Now try this!**

p 27
rectangle   triangle   pentagon   different hexagon

different triangle   different pentagon   7-sided shape   octagon

Now try this!

p 28
Encourage the children to be systematic:

□△○   ○△□   ○□△   △□○   △○□

(continued overleaf)

□○△□　○□△□　△□○□
□○□△　○□□△　△□□○
□□△○□　○□△□　□□△○□
□□△○　○□△□　□□△○
□□△○　△□□○　□○△□
□□○△　△□○□　□○□△
○△□□　△○□□　□□△○
○□△□　△○□□　□□○△

p 29
Now try this!

4	5	3
3	4	5
5	3	4

p 31
False
True
True
False

p 32
1. 16	**2.** 0	**3.** 20	**4.** 17
5. 14	**6.** 24	**7.** 9	**8.** 20

p 33
1. 24	**2.** 32	**3.** 30	**4.** 28
5. 11	**6.** 25	**7.** 13	**8.** 20

p 34
1. 8	**2.** 11	**3.** 9	**4.** 7
5. 5	**6.** 10	**7.** 6	**8.** 12

p 35
1. 9	**2.** 13	**3.** 29	**4.** 33
5. 4	**6.** 32	**7.** 66	**8.** 80

p 36
Mon 15　Tues 9　Wed 21　Thurs 16　Fri 14
Now try this!
30

p 37
Mon 19　Tues 9　Wed & Thurs 3　Fri 38
Now try this!
39　　67

p 38
1. 17	**2.** 8	**3.** 13
4. 9	**5.** 18	**6.** 14

Now try this!
6　　16

p 39
26　　14
37　　11
19

p 40
1. 65p	**2.** £1.25	**3.** £4.01	**4.** £1.31
5. £1.01	**6.** 62p	**7.** £1.28	**8.** £3.75

Now try this!
20p, 20p, 20p, 5p, 2p

p 41
50p + 20p + 2p
50p + 5p + 1p
20p + 10p + 2p + 1p
50p + 10p + 5p + 2p
50p + 20p + 10p + 5p + 2p + 1p
£1 + 10p
£2 + 20p + 10p
£2 + £1 + 1p
£2 + £1 + 5p + 1p

p 42
2
20
4
10
2
10
5
100
20

p 43
Now try this!
Oranges: 2 coins (£1, 10p)
Teabags: 4 coins (£2, 50p, 20p, 10p)
Toilet rolls: 3 coins (£2, £2, 50p)

p 44
1. 12p	**2.** 8p	**3.** 20p	**4.** 60p
5. 20p + 20p + 20p **or** 50p + 5p + 5p		**6.** 40p	

Now try this!
6p

p 45
1. 45p	**2.** £1.30	**3.** £1.50	**4.** £1 + 50p	**5.** 40p	**6.** 25p

Now try this!
11 paintbrushes

p 46
Stan = 8 cm　　　Dan = 24 cm　　　Brian = 6 cm
Tilly = 12 cm　　Mel = 16 cm

p 47
1. 68 cm	**2.** 80 cm	**3.** 1 m	**4.** 35 cm	**5.** 35 cm	**6.** 40 cm

Now try this!
Answers should be >80 cm <100 cm.

p 48
1. 150 g	**2.** 6	**3.** 8 kg	**4.** 6	**5.** 20 kg	**6.** 5

Now try this!
50 g

p 49
32 kg → 18 kg → 250 g → 16 kg → 60 kg
800 g ← 5 kg ← 8 g ← 3 kg ← 12 kg

p 50
1. 4	**2.** 60 litres	**3.** 70 litres	**4.** 4 litres	**5.** 10	**6.** 7

Now try this!
$1\frac{1}{2}$ litres

p 51
1. 15 litres	**2.** 3 bottles	**3.** 18 litres
4. 3 litres	**5.** 6 bottles	**6.** 21 litres

p 52
1. 10·30	**2.** 11·00	**3.** 8·45	**4.** 3·15
5. 7·15	**6.** 6·45	**7.** 8·30	**8.** 1·00

p 53
1. 9·30	**2.** 7·00	**3.** 3·15	**4.** 1·45
5. 7·15	**6.** 8·00	**7.** 11·30	**8.** 12·45

Now try this!
11·15　　11·45　　12·00

p 54
Even numbers under 20: 2, 4, 6, 8, 10, 12, 14, 16, 18
Multiples of 5 under 50: 5, 10, 15, 20, 25, 30, 35, 40, 45
Odd numbers from 16 to 32: 17, 19, 21, 23, 25, 27, 29, 31
Numbers below 10: 0, 1, 4, 7, 8
Numbers from 10 to 20: 11, 15, 16, 17, 19
Numbers above 20: 22, 29, 30

p 57
1. 2	**2.** Mushroom	**3.** 5	**4.** Cheese
5. Chicken	**6.** Beef	**7.** 11	**8.** Non-meat

p 58
1. 4	**2.** Pepperoni	**3.** Pepperoni	**4.** 18

p 59
1. 4	**2.** Green	**3.** Red
4. Grey	**5.** 3	**6.** 18

Now try this!
Blue and black, grey and green